1994

European
Vocational
Education
Systems

European Vocational Education Systems

A Guide to Vocational Education and Training in the European Community

Helen Collins

KOGAN PAGE

London • Philadelphia

First published in 1993

Apart from any fair dealing for the purposes of research or private study, or criticism or review, as permitted under the Copyright, Designs and Patents Act, 1988, this publication may only be reproduced, stored or transmitted, in any form or by any means, with the prior permission in writing of the publishers, or in the case of reprographic reproduction in accordance with the terms of licences issued by the Copyright Licensing Agency. Enquiries concerning reproduction outside those terms should be sent to the publishers at the undermentioned address:

Kogan Page Limited
120 Pentonville Road
London N1 9JN

© Helen Collins 1993

British Library Cataloguing in Publication Data

A CIP record for this book is available from the British Library.

ISBN 0 7494 0984 3

Typeset by Books Unlimited (Nottm), Sutton-in-Ashfield, NG17 1AL
Printed and bound in Great Britain by Biddles Ltd, Guildford and King's Lynn

Contents

Contents

Preface

THE PURPOSE OF THIS BOOK

There is now an extensive range of published literature available covering most areas in the field of education. However, there has not yet been any detailed and cohesive study which has sought to consider the different initiatives concerned with vocational education and training issues in the European Community. This guide should fill that gap. It has been planned to enable readers to put it to a variety of uses, depending on their perspective and activities concerning vocational education. All 12 vocational education systems have been presented as objectively as possible within national contexts, likewise no comparison between economic features and activity in member states is provided. In view of the extreme variation of educational and economic structures, any attempt at comparison would have forced a subjective bias, which would be counter to the book's aim to produce the facts and not the assumptions about each country.

WHO IS IT FOR?

The guide is intended to serve careers officers, advisers and careers teachers, VET practitioners, educational institutions, human resource managers, trainers and employers, as well as employees and students.

If you are a provider of guidance and advice on vocational training schemes and training initiatives it will:

- Inform you about the variety of issues that affect the provision of vocational training systems
- Enable you to examine the advice and guidance you may be providing against events happening in the rest of the EC
- Help you in considering and choosing appropriate advice and information

- Inform you about the background, tasks, competencies and skills required for successful mobility for professionals in the European Community.

If you are an employer or human resource manager it will:

- Act as a workplace tool to be used by employers and employees who are concerned with international exchanges of personnel, ideas, skills and expertise
- Provide the background information necessary to handle and initiate comparisons between employees' skills and qualifications originating in different member states
- Provide an insight into the wide variety of certificates and diplomas with which you are likely to be confronted
- Enable you to assess credentials issued within the contexts of widely different educational and training systems.

If you are interested in working in another EC country it will:

- Enable you to develop an overview of all the areas and issues involved in job hunting and employment
- Help you to decide what training you can pursue or qualifications you can provide
- Assist you in transferring your skills and qualifications to useful purpose in other member states or other occupational areas
- Help you to assess any training you are already undergoing and/or plan effective training related to future needs and qualifications.

For every reader it will:

- Provide frameworks and reference points, background material and sources of information
- Enable you to see patterns to prompt your thinking about your qualifications and work experience, so that you will cover all the important areas and not leave anything crucial out of account
- Provide you with enough background information to enable you to identify the credentials that are presented, place them in their educational context and make an informed assessment of their value.

HOW TO USE THE BOOK

All the country chapters follow the same model and are organized into six sections as follows:

— Key facts
— Education systems

— Vocational education systems
— Economic features
— Finding employment
— Information points

As the name suggests, the key facts charts show information about each member state such as its population, languages, political system, major towns, exports and imports. Sections two and three are concerned with education and vocational education systems in each country and provide information on compulsory education as well as on routes to further and higher education and qualifications obtained at each point. Both sections are designed to provide insight into the variety of structures within which vocational education is offered and the type of qualifications each system is geared to deliver. The fourth section, economic features, provides a description of the main characteristics and developments of each country's economy. Students and employees, as well as careers advisers and human resource managers concerned with providing appropriate information and advice will also benefit from section five, finding employment, since this section provides essential facts about working in each country as well as useful details about job search and job hunting in each member state. Given the constant changes and developments in the field of vocational education and training in the European Community, no guide of this nature can ever be absolutely complete; the final sections give a list of information points for those readers interested in finding out more about any particular aspect. The addresses of NARIC offices and comparability coordinators in each member state are provided in appendices at the back of the book.

Chapter 1

Introduction

VOCATIONAL TRAINING FOR THE 1990s

Economic uncertainty, turbulence and restructuring are the European Commission's forecasts for the future. The response: continuing change by industry and the EC's institutions through a reinforced education and training programme. Current demographic trends are expected to continue. As fewer young workers are coming onto the labour market, the skills training of the adult population will become increasingly important. Over 80 per cent of the year 2000's workforce is already on the labour market. While the skill-base needs to be renewed by between 10 and 15 per cent per year, the annual entry of young people into the labour market accounts for only 2 per cent of the active workforce.

Multiple qualifications are increasingly being demanded by industry; with this in mind the organization of work must also change. The rigid division between technical skills and management skills, for example, is becoming outdated. It is clear that training bodies have to adjust and combine their technical training with management and social training while companies have to examine how they organize work. In light of these new demands on vocational education and the labour market, in 1990 the Commission proposed a three-pronged action plan to meet the potential challenges of the 1990s:

- Investment in training must be increased, and access to and participation in appropriate vocational training should be made easier. All young people should have broadly-based and recognized qualifications and there should be access to training throughout working life.
- The quality of training needs to improve to meet the growth in training needs. The Commission forecast that this could be done through exchange of information and experience through, for example, the transnational mobility of trainers and trainees and the development of distance learning.
- Equal access to vocational training needs to be guaranteed by

removing all discrimination on the grounds of nationality. This means that diplomas, certificates and other qualifications have to be mutually recognized and acknowledged.

To enforce this three-pronged plan, the Commission has built on its many training action programmes. EC training programmes are concentrated around five key areas: initial training, higher education, continuing training, language training and training done in conjunction with non-EC countries like Eastern Europe, EFTA countries (Austria, Finland, Iceland, Liechtenstein, Norway, Sweden and Switzerland) and developing countries.

In most industrialized countries, the education and training market resembles a giant orange, most of which is consumed by compulsory basic education. Higher education and universities then account for quite a few segments, rendered attractive by the official recognition of the certificates awarded and the access they provide to professional jobs. Until recently, the number of segments awarded to vocational training or anything involving the training of workers on or off the job has been very small. However, the consumers of vocational education are, in effect, the entire working population, or to put it another way, the life-blood of the European Community's economy. Today, the trend in education seems to be one of continuing education and training, and increasingly it is becoming regarded as a life-long process that benefits both employers and individuals alike.

The important role of small and medium sized enterprises (SMEs), which account for over 80 per cent of Community business, is also acknowledged by the European Commission as a priority training area for the European Community.

TRAINING PROVISIONS IN THE MAASTRICHT TREATY

The important role of vocational training to meet the challenges brought about by industrial change and to facilitate labour market integration was clearly recognized in the Treaty on European Political Union agreed at Maastricht in December 1991.

Developing exchanges and expertise, promoting trainer and trainee mobility, enhancing cooperation between training organizations and the business and industrial worlds and cooperation between specialized organizations in non-EC countries were seen as key action areas of EC policy.

The text on vocational training agreed in the Treaty includes:

1. The Community shall implement a vocational training policy which shall support and supplement the action of Member States, while

fully respecting the responsibility of Member States for the content and organization of vocational training.

2. Community action shall aim to:
    – facilitate adaptation to industrial changes in particular through vocational training and retraining;
    – improve initial and continuing vocational training in order to facilitate vocational integration and reintegration into the labour market;
    – facilitate access to vocational training and encourage mobility of instructors and trainees, particularly young people;
    – stimulate cooperation on training between educational/ training establishments and business/commerce;
    – develop exchanges of information and experience on issues common to the training systems of the Member States.
3. The Community and the Member States shall foster cooperation between the competent international organizations in the sphere of vocational training.
4. The Council shall adopt measures to contribute to the achievement of the objectives.

In examining European vocational educational systems it is important to pay attention to the five principal objectives which the European Community has identified as its policy for vocational education and training over the period 1990–1995. These are:

1. A multi-cultural and multi-lingual Europe.
2. A mobile workforce.
3. A Europe of training for all.
4. A Europe of skills.
5. A Europe open to the world.

The Treaty of Rome enshrines the freedom to work anywhere in the Community, and early on the Community determined to remove the obstacle of new professional qualifications having to be gained in a country where the person wished to practise. This used to mean that professional people needed to obtain appropriate professional qualifications before they had the right to work or practise in another country. The first phase of tackling this was through agreements on common standards of qualification, either through an agreed minimum (*harmonization*) or through mutual recognition. In this way *Sectoral Directives* were adopted for nurses, doctors, veterinary surgeons, architects, dentists, general practitioners, and to some extent, the legal profession.

By 1985 it became very clear that this profession-by-profession approach would take forever. Therefore, a new approach was proposed by the European Commission, and a *General Directive* was adopted in late 1988 for implementation by January 1991. For all professions regulated in some way by the state and requiring at least three years' higher education, it was agreed that a professional status (for example, chartered engineer, qualified school teacher, etc) gained in one country in the EC would be recognized in all of the others. The network of National Academic Recognition Information Centres in each Member State plays a key role in identifying the academic equivalence of qualifications gained in different Member States.

To practise in another country, a person does not have to re-qualify, though there are various safeguards built in to ensure that a Danish engineer, for example, has the appropriate knowledge and experience to be effective in other countries.

Only Ireland met the implementation deadline, but the UK and Denmark soon followed in April and May 1991 respectively. The General Directive covers many professions including engineering, law, teaching, ophthalmic optics, many of the health professions and chartered surveying. A second Council directive was introduced in 1992 for the recognition of professional education and training to supplement directive 89/48.

The first Directive was limited to professionals who had undergone a period of higher education; the second Directive increases mobility for many other individuals. It was agreed by the Commission that in order to facilitate the pursuit of all professional activities which in a host Member State are dependent on the completion of a certain level of education and training, a second general system was necessary to complement the first. The second Directive applies to regulated occupations which require for the purposes of entry either higher education of between one and three years' duration (Diploma), or other post-secondary level education plus training (Certificate). It also takes into account recognized work experience.

Together, these Directives give every Community national certain rights to have qualifications and experience gained in one Member State recognized or taken into account in other Member States where entry to particular jobs is regulated on the basis of specific national qualifications. Such regulations may be direct or indirect, by virtue of laws, regulations or administrative provisions. In practice, the Directives aim to ensure that, where a perosn is qualified to pursue a profession in one Member State, there are no unnecessary barriers to their practising that profession in other Member States.

COMPARABILITY OF VOCATIONAL QUALIFICATIONS

As far as comparability of vocational qualifications in the EC is concerned, the main responsibility lies with the European Centre for the

Development of Vocational Training, known as CEDEFOP. The end of 1992 marked the creation of a single European market. Barriers to trade between the Member States have been removed, encouraging free movement in the Community of goods, services, capital and labour. The Comparability of Vocational Qualifications initiative is contributing to making this a reality through assisting the mobility of labour by:

- encouraging individuals to make better use of the qualifications for the purposes of gaining better access to employment in another Member State
- helping employers to make more informed comparisons between vocational qualifications in use in the European Community.

The general principles for implementing a common vocational training policy were adopted in 1963. In the 1970s and early 1980s some technical comparison work was carried out by CEDEFOP. However, it was not until 1985 that a more committed and systematic approach was set in motion through a European Council Decision of 16 July. CEDEFOP is located in Berlin with a staff of some 60 people who are recruited from all Member States. It is not simply an agent for the Commission. Its general policy is laid down by quadripartite representation from:

- Member governments
- European Commission
- Trade unions
- Employers.

The centre's three major functions are to act as:

- a pioneer and initiator of innovations;
- a forum for the exchange of information and experience among the most important players in vocational training (the social partners, governments, national and international institutions);
- a support institution assisting the Commission of the European Communities.

CEDEFOP has agencies in each Member State which act as a focus for the dissemination of information on issues of vocational education and training.

TRANSPARENCY OF QUALIFICATION SYSTEMS

An EC Council Resolution on the *transparency* of qualifications was passed in 1992, outlining the need for new forms of action by the European Community and Member States to encourage the free movement of labour. The need for new initiatives to promote the free movement of labour reflects the fact that most of the comparability work that has taken place to date does not go far enough in providing the kind of clear details about qualifications necessary to promote free movement of labour.

The aim of transparency initiatives is to enable individuals to present their education, vocational qualifications and work experience simply and effectively to potential employers throughout the EC, and for employers to have simple and straightforward access to clear descriptions of qualifications in order to establish the relevance of applicants' skills and qualifications to the type of jobs available. This approach raises the question of making available individual records providing a summary of achievements in a common format agreed between Member States; it will also involve much greater emphasis on information exchanges between those organizations concerned with approving and awarding qualifications to uphold the objective of transparency. It may also involve some transfer of data and networking between national databases in different Member States.

The focus and debate on transparency of qualifications is particularly important in view of the significance placed within the EC on the principle of 'subsidiarity'. To ensure that national systems are not disadvantaged by an over-centralized approach, and to allow maximum input from national institutions, it is vital that new ways be found to encourage greater understanding of national systems on their own terms.

EUROQUALIFICATION

EUROQUALIFICATION is a new training course that has been developed jointly by partner organizations in the Member States and the European Community. It promotes the right to free movement of workers, partnerships between companies and social dialogue. The main aims of EUROQUALIFICATION are to:

- Train people to carry out their occupation in partnership and/or in occupational mobility situations.
- Lend a European, vocational and linguistic dimension to the training needs of over 6000 people in some 40 selected occupations in 12 occupational fields:
  - car repair / vehicle maintenance
  - catering / hotel trade / tourism
  - commerce
  - construction
  - electricity/ electronics / telecommunications
  - environment / local development
  - food processing industry

  - – graphics industry
  - – mechanics
  - – office automation
  - – textiles
  - – transport.
- Ensure greater coherence and convergence of Community vocational training programmes.
- Ensure joint and/or mutual recognition of the newly attained qualifications: vocational, linguistic, transnational.
- Make this joint approach an original and transferable experience for national and Community organizations and to ensure that it has good prospects for expansion.

Access to EUROQUALIFICATION is free of charge for the target groups: young people and the long-term unemployed, prepared to be mobile in the framework of their training, and people employed in insecure work situations.

For further information about EUROQUALIFICATION contact the central office in Brussels; the address is in Appendix 1.

Chapter 2

Belgium

KEY FACTS

Surface area	30,510 sq km, 11,780 sq miles
Capital	Brussels
Major towns	Ghent, Liège, Charleroi, Bruges, Mons, Namur, Leuven; ports are Antwerp, Ostend, Zeebrugge
Form of government	liberal democracy
Population	(1990 est) 9,895,000; annual growth rate 0.1 per cent
Languages	in the North (Flanders) Flemish (a Dutch dialect, known as Vlaams) 55 per cent; in the South (Wallonia) Walloon (a French dialect) 32 per cent; bilingual 11 per cent; German (Eastern border) 0.6 per cent; all are official
Currency	Belgian franc
Exports	iron, steel, textiles, manufactured goods, petrochemicals
Vocational educational institutions	technical or vocational institutes; adult vocational training centres; Community and Regional Office for Vocational Training and Employment (FOREM); Flemish Employment and Training Service (VDAB)

Awarding organizations	Ministry of Education, Research and Training; FOREM; Ministry for the Flemish Community
Grants	students in post-compulsory education and undergraduates can qualify for a means-tested grant; interest-free loans can also be obtained to supplement or in lieu of a grant
Vocational qualifications	certificate or diploma on completion of training
Trends/developments	several new training centres are under development

EDUCATION SYSTEM

The complex organization of the education system in Belgium reflects the linguistic and religious diversity; the two Education Ministries cover the French- (plus the German minority) and the Dutch-speaking areas respectively. Over half of all school pupils attend the private Catholic sector; private schools are heavily subsidized by public funds. Compulsory schooling lasts from 6 to 14, but most children attend both pre- and post-compulsory education. Compulsory education can be extended to the age of 16 if a child has not completed his or her first two-year cycle of secondary education; and there is compulsory part-time education for pupils aged between 16 and 18, principally those who will not be following secondary education. Over 95 per cent of children aged 3–5 pre-primary schooling, mostly in state nursery schools (*école maternelle/kleuterschool*). These schools are open 8.30–15.30, with a one hour lunch break, and are closed on Wednesday afternoons.

Primary education

Primary education is provided by the state for 6–12 year olds in primary schools, (*école primaire/babischool*) in three two-year cycles. The curriculum is broadly defined and the emphasis is on a child-centred approach. The syllabus includes mother tongue, mathematics, environmental studies, activities involving self-expression, religious studies and physical education. The second national language is compulsory in Brussels from the third year, but is a fifth-year option elsewhere.

Secondary education

After age 12 the secondary system commences (*école secondaire/middelbareschool*). Secondary education is based on a comprehensive system and lasts for six years, divided into three two-year cycles. All public sector schools were changed following the educational reforms in 1978. In the Catholic (private) sector, reform has proceeded more slowly. The traditional system is divided into four specialized fields:

- general (academic);
- artistic;
- technical; or
- vocational education.

In general schools, pupils must specialize in the first cycle for either the Latin or the modern section (including science). Compulsory subjects are mother tongue, history, geography, mathematics, a first foreign language, biology, art, physical education and Latin. In the second cycle, further choices are possible: Latin with either Greek, mathematics or sciences, Sciences A (mathematics, physics), Sciences B (natural sciences) and economics. The various subjects are taught separately. The other types of school each have a basic core of secondary subjects, with extra subjects appropriate to the school type. The reformed system has adopted a multidisciplinary approach, with all pupils attending the same type of school. Complete specialization is deferred until the third two-year cycle.

Pupils are grouped within the school into the same four categories as in the traditional system, but for most of the first cycle, classes are held in common and this practice continues for a few subjects until the final year. Some specialization begins in the third year, but transfers between categories are still possible up to the fourth year. Pupils can choose from a wide range of options to build up a balanced but individual education. In the first year, pupils must study either a first foreign language or the other national language. Under the reformed system, continuous assessment replaces the traditional pattern of bi-annual examinations.

Special education

Special education is provided in separate schools at each level, including some with boarding facilities for children with physical disabilities. Eight types of disability are defined, covering various types of physical or learning handicap, including behavioural problems. Before a child is registered for special education an expert report is produced in consultation with his or her family. In Belgium, integrated education exists for motor and sensory disabled pupils and pupils with instrumental or behavioural difficulties.

Administration

Two Ministries administer education and culture, the Ministry for National Education and French Culture (covering also the German-speaking minority) and the Ministry for National Education and Dutch Culture. A joint Secretary-General coordinates the two Ministries, and frequent meetings are held.

Several different authorities are responsible for schools, namely the state, the provinces, the municipalities and private bodies (usually Catholic).

Technical education is organized mainly at provisional level and primary education at municipal. All state subsidized schools must meet certain conditions concerning inspection and minimum standards. An authority can use the state curricula or submit its own for approval by the Ministry. Inspectors, recruited by examination, are usually responsible for a specific subject and aid curricula reform.

Finance

Since the late 1970s, about 6 per cent of Belgium's GNP has been spent on education, excluding provincial, municipal and Church expenditure. Subsidies to the private school system amount to over half of the total budget, as the state pays all teachers' salaries. No fees are payable in public or recognized private schools.

Pupils in post-compulsory schooling and undergraduates can qualify for a means-tested grant or scholarship, depending on the nature of their studies. Interest-free loans can also be obtained, to supplement or in lieu of a grant. Foreign students in higher education pay much higher tuition fees than nationals, although a small number of grants and scholarships are reserved specifically for students from other EC countries.

VOCATIONAL EDUCATION SYSTEM

Post-compulsory education

The final years in the secondary school, from age 15 to 18, are post-compulsory. Since 1983 young people must remain at school until the age of 18, either in full-time education or on part-time courses. The latter incorporate a wide range of options for students to select the form and method of study or training that suits them best. Pupils successfully completing secondary education receive a certificate, at either the lower or the higher level. Those wishing to enter a short-term higher education course must have achieved a *certificat de l'enseignement secondaire supérieur* (CESS) or a *getuigschrift van hoger secundair onderwijs* (GHSO), which are the official approved certificates of higher secondary education awarded after a duration of study of 12 years: six years of primary education and six years of secondary education. They are awarded by an educational institution in general, technical or secondary education or by a state examination board for secondary education.

Transition from school to work

Some types of secondary education are specifically vocational or technical. At the end of primary schooling pupils can transfer either to a grammar school-type of education or to a vocational/technical type. At the end of the fourth or fifth year of secondary technical education students are awarded a vocational certificate, skills certificate or apprenticeship certificate, depending on the nature of their studies, the level they reached and the length of time it took them to complete the syllabus. The qualification obtained can lead to a number of options including further study (either full- or part-time), employment with on-going day-release to convert school qualifications into higher level certificates, or vocational training.

Pupils leaving school at 14 can enter a four-year apprenticeship, with day release, leading to a professional certificate in a whole range of occupational areas including engineering, construction crafts, hairdressing, clerical skills, catering, etc. Eighteen-year-olds with these certificates or an appropriate school qualification can attend evening classes for up to three years, to attempt an advanced certificate course. After age 18, students can continue their studies by a variety of means including evening schools, distance learning and correspondence courses, employer in-house training schemes or full-time higher education.

Higher education

Some 0.2 million students enrol annually in higher education, either in one of the 19 universities or in a non-university comprising various specialized types of college, eg technology, paramedical, teacher training, art, hotel management, travel and tourism.

The entry qualifications to university education are:

- *Diplôme d'aptitude á acceder à l'enseignement supérieur* (DAES)/*Bekwaamheids-diploma dat toegang verleent tot het hoger onderwijs* (BDHO);

- *Diplôme d'enseignement supérieur de type court/Diploma van hoger onderwijs van het korte type* with complete curriculum;
- *Diplôme de licencié/Diploma van handelsingenieur* or *d'ingénieur commercial/van handelsingenieur* (commercial engineering);
- *Diplôme d'ingénieur technicien/Diploma van technisch ingeniéur* (technical engineer);
- *Diplôme de l'examen d'admission aux études de candidat/Diploma van het toelatingsexamen voor de opleiding van kandidaat* (diploma for access to the examination of *candidat/kandidaat*):
  - in civil engineering;
  - in agricultural engineering;
  - in the sciences (mathematics and physics).

University courses are divided into three cycles.

- The first cycle: after two years or four semesters, the *candidat/kandidaat* is awarded. A feature of the first cycle is the general character of the subjects taught.
- The second cycle: after two, three or five years of specialized training, the following degrees are awarded:
  - Diploma of *licencié/licentiaat*
  - Diploma of *pharmacien/apotheker*
  - Diploma of *ingénieur/ingenieur*
  - Diploma of *docteur/doctor*.

The second cycle also includes the *agrégation de l'enseignement secondaire supérieur*; holders are qualified to teach in secondary schools and in non-university short-term higher education institutions.

- The third cycle, lasting from one year upwards, leads to the following degrees:
  - *docteur/doctor*
  - *agrégé de l'enseignement supérieur*, or *docteur spécial/speciaal doctor* (the highest university degree).

Progress in higher education is monitored by annual examinations, which those failing can re-sit only once. Courses are long, four to six years at least, beginning with two or three years' general study, progressing to more specialized work including a final thesis to obtain the licence. A doctorate requires two or three years more study and the highest qualification (*agrégé de l'enseignement supérieur*) requires another two years to present an original dissertation, three extra theses and a lecture.

Non-university education

Non-university education comprises either short or long courses. Short courses require the upper secondary certificate, last for two or three years and lead to a final diploma which qualifies the holder for immediate employment. The wide variety of occupations/subjects which can be studied at this level include nursing, business studies, librarianship, social work, technical engineering, pre-school and primary school teaching and some lower secondary school subject teachers.

Teacher training

Teacher training courses focus on a particular level of education: pre-school, primary or lower secondary in two year courses at teacher training colleges, while upper secondary teachers are university graduates, who mainly qualify simultaneously in both sectors. Higher education lecturers must have the highest qualification (*agrégé de l'enseignement supérieur*) described above. Each local authority determines its own in-service training for teachers in a variety of ways.

Adult education

Provision is made at both secondary and higher education levels, as evening classes or by correspondence. Since 1973, Belgian workers are entitled to paid study leave. A variety of courses exist, often linked with universities. A number of positive action programmes have been introduced to combat long-term unemployment among women; as part of these measures women's education has become a major priority of the Ministry of Education.

ECONOMIC FEATURES

Although Belgium is one of the smallest countries in Europe, it has a population of around ten million and is the most densely populated country in the EC after The Netherlands. Language is an important issue, with Belgium politically divided along linguistic lines. Flanders is the Dutch-speaking region and Wallonia the French. Brussels is officially a bilingual and politically separate 'island' surrounded by Flanders. There is also an area along Belgium's eastern border with Germany, known as Eastern Cantons, where German is spoken. The people of Flanders refer to their language as either Flemish or Dutch. Flanders covers the northern half of Belgium and consists of four provinces: West-Vlaanderen, Oost-Vlaanderen, Antwerpen and Limburg. The four French-speaking Walloon provinces in the south of Belgium are: Hainaut, Namur, Luxembourg and Liège. The ninth province, Brabant, has been divided into three districts: Halle-Vilvoorde (Dutch-speaking), Nivelles (French-speaking) and Brussels (bilingual). Brussels is divided into administrative areas called communes which all have their own police department and town hall.

Employment promotion measures

In March 1990, a cooperation programme known as *Plan 1+1=3* was signed. This was an initiative of the national Ministry of Employment and Labour. All competent authorities (national, regional and community) now participate in this plan which aims to maximize the chances of economic reintegration of the long-term unemployed (LTUs). A *Round Table Fund* was created so as to ensure the necessary financial support, and a transfer of BFR 150 million was made to this fund from the budget of the national Ministry of Employment and Labour. With these funds, grants are awarded for certain initiatives which aim to reintegrate the LTUs.

Initiators of projects with whom the Minister of Employment and Labour has a cooperation agreement on projects to foster the integration of LTUs are eligible for premium funding. The Royal Decree of 5 September 1991 stipulates the conditions and modalities for granting these premiums and has extended the range of measures to allow other groups at risk among the unemployed to benefit, to include the following categories:

- jobseekers who have received unemployment benefit (or waiting allowance) for every day of the week for at least the year preceding the implementation of the integration;
- jobseekers who are registered at the National Fund for the social Rehabilitation of the Disabled;
- persons receiving minimum subsistence benefit who are registered as jobseekers;
- registered jobseekers who wish to integrate or reintegrate into the employment market and who at the same time satisfy certain conditions which stipulate that:
  - they must not have worked during the three years prior to their integration; and
  - they must not have received unemployment benefit, waiting allowance or career break allowance; or
  - during the aforementioned period of three years, they have interrupted their career or not worked at all in order to either bring up their children or to care for a parent; or
  - they must be jobseekers whose entitlement to unemployment benefits is suspended because of an exceptionally long period of unemployment.

Beneficiaries of the premium

Only those initiators of projects which have been approved may receive the premium, namely:

- the Brussels Regional Employment Office (ORBEM), the National Employment Office (ONEM), the Walloon Community and Regional Vocational Training and Employment Service (FOREM) and the Flemish Office of Employment and Vocational Training (VDAB);
- an enterprise or a group of enterprises, a subsistence insurance fund, an association installed by an organization, any part of the public sector which has concluded an agreement with one of the aforementioned bodies.

Projects

Initiatives to promote the integration of LTUs involve operational programmes consisting of the following elements:

- a general description of the programme;
- a quantitative and qualitative description of the categories of jobseekers targeted in the programme;
- the way in which the programme supports the chances of integration in the work circuit or increases the employment prospects of those jobseekers concerned;
- a description of the tasks of those participants associated with the programme;
- the duration and place of the action;
- evaluation of the costs of the action;
- modalities of evaluation and control.

In order to obtain the premium, the initiator of the project must submit the operational programme to the Ministry of Employment and Labour. The Evaluation Commission then passes judgement on the programme. The decision, which is reached unanimously by the members present, must be made known within two months of the application being made. The Minister of Employment and Labour signs a cooperation agreement with the project initiator, following the Evaluation Commission's recommendations. The cooperation agreement includes the operational programme and stipulates the amount of funding to be awarded.

Job creation

Recruitment premium in the Brussels-Capital region

Since 1 November 1991, employers in the Brussels-Capital region can benefit from a recruitment premium when hiring LTUs or young persons with little schooling. The premium is awarded by the Brussels Regional Employment Office (ORBEM).

Employers concerned
An enterprise which has its head office or place of business in the Brussels-Capital region can apply for the premium. Besides this, to be eligible for the premium, the enterprise must:

- have informed ORBEM of the vacancy;
- hire the jobseeker on the basis of a permanent employment contract;
- have satisfied the requirements relating to youth traineeships;
- employ the worker in the Brussels-Capital region.

Furthermore, the recruitment must correspond to a net employment increase in the enterprise. The premium may be temporarily reserved for certain categories of enterprise on the basis of a shortage of personnel in a particular sector.

Workers concerned
In order to be eligible for the premium, jobseekers must be unemployed and registered at ORBEM. The jobseekers must satisfy certain conditions when they are hired. There are four categories of jobseekers:

- young persons aged between 18 and 25 years with little schooling;
- jobseekers aged under 35 years who have been unemployed for at least 24 months during the four years prior to being hired;
- jobseekers aged 35 years and over who have been unemployed during the 12 months prior to being hired;
- disabled jobseekers who have been unemployed during the 12 months prior to being hired.

Amount of premium
The premium is BFR 15,000 per month for a full-time job for either half-time or part-time. It is granted for a maximum period of 12 months. The number of jobseekers for whom the enterprise may receive the premium is limited to:

- one when its workforce is fewer than 10 employees;
- two when the workforce is between 10 and 19 employees;
- 10 per cent of its personnel when the workforce is 20 employees or more.

Employment promotion for groups which are at risk
Since 1989 various employment programme laws have stipulated that certain employers must sign collective agreements which reserve a

percentage of the wage bill for employment promotion of groups among the unemployed which are at risk. The 1993–4 contribution stands at 0.25·per cent of the wage bill. Of this amount, 0.1 per cent must be set aside for the most vulnerable of the groups which are at risk.

Enterprises which are not bound by a collective agreement must make an equivalent contribution to the Employment Fund. The total sum of these contributions is allocated to other initiatives to promote the vocational integration of groups which are at risk by financing new projects. The Royal Decree of 23 September 1991 and the Ministerial Decree of 4 November 1991 implementing the Royal Decree specify the modalities of allocation of the 0.25 per cent contribution.

Projects

The Employment Fund may provide financing directly to the employers, in the framework of individual make-work projects for persons belonging to the groups which are at risk, to promoters of collective projects as stated in collective agreements which affect a number of persons from groups which are at risk.

Projects can therefore be considered which are put forward by sectors, enterprises or groups of enterprises, and in some cases in cooperation with the regional and community employment and vocational training offices (FOREM, VDAB or ORBEM) and which:

- exceed the overall target of 0.25 per cent of the wage bill;
- include positive action measures for women;
- come from sectors, enterprises or groups of enterprises which, not being bound by a collective agreement, have made the equivalent contribution of 0.25 per cent to the Employment Fund.

Vocational Integration Agreement

Individual or collective projects are implemented by the employer or promoter in the framework of a *Vocational Integration Agreement*. This agreement lasts for between six months and one year. It must be signed by the Minister of Employment and Labour after the Evaluation Commission has passed judgement. This Commission consists of a president, two secretaries and employers' and workers' representatives. It also includes representatives of the regional and community Ministries who are responsible for employment, training and education. The Commission has a period of two months in which to pass judgement; the Minister must adhere to the finding if it was reached unanimously. As soon as the signed agreement is received, the employer or project promoter proceeds to implement the project and hires those persons it is designed to help. Employment must be on the basis of a permanent employment contract or a youth traineeship contract.

Financial support

The financial support provided by the Employment Fund is laid down in the *Vocational Integration Agreement* and depends on the nature of the project, the initiator and, if relevant, the profile of the jobseekers concerned. For individual make-work projects, it amounts to a maximum of BFR 30,000 or BFR 15,000 per month and per jobseeker. For collective agreements, support is set at a maximum of BFR 406,224 per year and per person concerned in the project. In the case of collective projects which include positive action measures for women, the financial support corresponds to the actual costs of the project which have been laid down in a collective agreement.

New employment incentives in the Walloon region

The Regional Walloon Executive has adopted two decrees within the framework of *Programme Plus* (a long-term programme of revitalization of Wallonia, covering several sectors). By means of subsidies, one decree aims to promote the hiring of jobseekers for training, and the other aims to foster the employment of jobseekers who are difficult to place.

Training measures

The decree which concerns the employment of jobseekers applies to industrial or commercial enterprises with a place of business in the Walloon Region. However, it excludes enterprises involved in the production and distribution of energy, or those in the tertiary sector dealing with the wholesale or retail distribution of goods and services. Three incentives are planned, these are respectively:

* Enterprises intending to train employees receive an employment and training subsidy when they hire persons who are unemployed and registered at the Community and Regional Vocational Training and Employment Service (FOREM) or in a similar situation to jobseekers, namely:
  – persons in part-time employment whose working hours amount to one-third of the normal working hours for full-time work in the same company;
  – elderly unemployed;
  – unemployed persons working at a sheltered workplace, etc.

The amount of subsidy is related to the length of the period for which the jobseeker has been out of work, prior to being hired. This amounts to:
  – BFR 50,000 for hiring a jobseeker who has been unemployed for up to six months;

- BFR 75,000 for hiring a jobseeker who has been unemployed for between six months and one year;
- BFR 100,000 for hiring a jobseeker who has been unemployed for more than one year.

- FOREM will contribute towards selection and training costs for personnel appointed to replace workers who have been transferred to new production plants. This is granted on the condition that when trained, workers are taken on, after they have been unemployed for at least six consecutive months. Furthermore, they must be:
  - nationals of an EC Member State or resident in the Walloon region;
  - at least 18 years old; and
  - employed by an enterprise on a permanent labour contract.

FOREM will cover 50 per cent of the expenses declared by the employer; this includes an undertaking to partially and temporarily reimburse the wage costs of the training instructors and of those who receive the training.

- FOREM will also cover some of the costs inherent in the selection and training of personnel who are recruited to fill a position requiring lower qualifications, as a direct or indirect consequence of the application of new technology. This subsidy is of the same nature as the previous subsidy. It is also limited to 50 per cent of the expenses declared by the employer; it is subject to the same conditions (nationality, residence, age, etc); however, in this case, the jobseeker must be registered as such for a period of 12 months.

Employment measures

The second decree concerns the hiring of jobseekers who are difficult to place. It applies to individuals or legal entities who have a place of business in the Walloon region and who offer permanent employment to a person both registered and resident in the Walloon region who is:

- either an unemployed person who is in receipt of full benefit, but not a jobseeker (ie, an elderly unemployed person, with a reduced capacity to work or exempted for family and social reasons);
- or a jobseeker registered at FOREM, meeting one of the following criteria:
  - be in a period of compulsory part-time education;
  - be between 18 and 25 years old, be considered as a person with few qualifications and be registered as a jobseeker for a period of at least 12 months;
  - be at least 40 years old and be registered as a jobseeker for a period of 12 months;

- receive minimum subsistence wages for at least three months, except for those cases where the minimum wages have been granted following a refusal to work as a result of insufficient or reduced learning or physical capacities;
- be in part-time employment, whereby the working hours are equivalent to less than one-third of the normal working hours for full-time work in the same company;
- be employed at a sheltered workplace or follow vocational training, organized or approved by FOREM or by the National Fund for the Social Rehabilitation of the Disabled.

The decree grants a subsidy, for a maximum of four quarters, which is equal to BFR 40,000 per quarter for full-time work, or a proportion of the amount for part-time work. Payment of the subsidy is subject to the following conditions:

- at the end of each of the first three quarters during which FOREM funding is given, the number of workers registered at the end of the three corresponding quarters of the previous year must be at least as many units (ie, workers) as there are grants approved (a maximum of four per employer). As far as the last quarter of FOREM funding is concerned, the number must be at least equal to that registered at the end of the quarter during which the hiring took place;
- additional jobs resulting from the hirings maintained for two years, as of the date of the first quarter of FOREM funding. Proof of the continued employment of workers for whom the subsidy was granted is established by means of a list of names submitted to the ONSS at the end of each of the eight quarters concerned.

However, it should be noted that certain employers are not eligible for a *Plus* Subsidy. This applies in particular to public legal entities and educational institutes, enterprises without industrial or commercial purposes, temporary work agencies and certain professions.

Special projects for LTUs in Flanders

Projects which provide training and guidance for LTUs can be classified as follows:

- Training focused directly on the employment market:
  - technical training,
  - pre-training,
  - basic training,
  - retraining,
  - advanced training,
  - individual training in companies,

- training in jobsearch techniques or jobclubs.
- Training focused indirectly on the employment market:
  - projects of integration training (*formations d'insertion/ schakelopleidingen*);
  - other training projects focusing on specific target groups; eg, recently arrived immigrants, workers with disabilities, the homeless, etc.
- Vocational guidance and orientation:
  - *Weer-werk* action (back to work).

Weer-werk is aimed at LTUs, ie, persons who have been unemployed for longer than one year or who receive a minimum allowance from the General Centre for Social Work, CPAS. A 1990 survey conducted by CPAS shed some light on the problem of the long-term unemployed and revealed that:

- there is a disproportionately high number of persons with very little education; half of the LTUs have received basic secondary education;
- 65 to 80 per cent of LTUs are women;
- male LTUs are generally older and less educated than female LTUs;
- participation of LTUs in the positive developments in the labour market in the late 1980s was negligible.

Objectives of Weer-werk

The aim of the *Weer-werk* is to accompany and guide LTUs into lasting work. That can be accomplished directly or indirectly (through training, assistance, etc). Since it was introduced, an ongoing collaborative survey of the target group's needs in relation to employment and training has been undertaken by the groups involved. Some important principles are inherent in this accompaniment:

- an individual approach: the problems of unemployment are not the same for everyone; accompaniment must be made-to-measure;
- a permanent approach: the reintegration of LTUs will rarely be acheived after just one meeting; this reintegration will often require a long process of accompaniment;
- participation in the *Weer-werk* plan is voluntary; jobseekers will be informed of this new possibility. Non-participation cannot be penalized;
- the target group is analysed; its size and profile are known. Relying on a number of criteria, priorities can be set as regards the target group. On this basis, grading can then be established;
- information and motivation: LTUs are informed of *Weer-werk* projects through the media and trade unions. On a local level, organizations, associations and persons in contact with the target

group are informed of and if possible involved in recruitment. In this way, candidates can apply voluntarily, or receive a written invitation to participate in the project. An appointment is made with each prospective candidate for an introductory interview. A *reintegration protocol* is signed by the vocational counsellor and the client, and is a concise, written account of the plan of action which summarizes the moral obligation of both parties.

All project activities are organized either in centres of the Flemish Office of Employment and Vocational Training (VDAB) or by the VDAB in collaboration with employing organizations or training bodies. Since 1989, new collaborative efforts to benefit LTUs have been set up between the Community Minister of Employment, the VDAB and various industrial sectors (lumber, clothing, construction, hotel and catering, and food). The VDAB has undertaken to train a set number of LTUs for these sectors. For their part, the industrial sectors undertake to mediate with their companies to take on these persons after their training. Under the auspices of the Community Minister of Employment, the respective sectors and the VDAB are leading an 'information and consciousness-raising campaign' to publicize the VDAB training courses which are relevant for these sectors. All of these sectoral initiatives are part of a Belgium-wide effort to earmark 0.25 per cent of the wage bill for training and employing high-risk groups.

FINDING EMPLOYMENT

EC nationals have the right to live and work in Belgium without a work permit. However, a full EC passport is essential; a visitor's passport or excursion document is not sufficient. EC nationals are free to enter Belgium for up to three months to look for work or set up in business. There is a compulsory social security scheme for self-employed people, which should be joined no later than 90 days after starting work in Belgium.

Anyone arriving in Belgium to look for work must register at the local town hall (*maison communale* or *gemeentehuis*) within eight days of arrival. Visitors receive a *Certificate d'Immatriculation* (a temporary residence permit), which is valid for three months, or a one-year permit, *Certificat d'Inscription au Registre d'Etrangers* (CIRE). In some cases, temporary residence permits may be renewed for a further three months before a CIRE is awarded. Children must also be registered for residence purposes. Children under the age of 12 receive a name card while those aged 12–15 are issued with either a name card or a child's identity card, at the discretion of the parent.

EC nationals have the same rights as Belgian nationals with regard to pay, working conditions, access to housing, vocational education and training, social security and trade union membership. EC nationals have free access to the services of the Belgian employment services, which are:

in Flanders: *Vlaamse Dienst voor Arbeidsbemiddeling* (VDAB)
in Wallonia: *Office de la Formation Professionelle de l'Emploi* (FOREM)
in Brussels: *Office Régional Bruxellois et de l'Emploi* (BDGA/ORBEM).

Because Belgian labour law gives employees extensive rights after 12 months' service, many employers prefer to employ workers on temporary contracts. Temporary contracts usually run for five or six weeks after satisfactory completion of a three-day trial period. Private employment agencies are listed in the main Belgian business telephone directories, *Pages d'Or/Gouden Gids,* under *Bureaux de Placement/Aanwevingsbureaus* (permanent work) or *Intérimaires/Tijdelijke Arbeid* (temporary work). Large public reference libraries in other EC countries often hold copies of *Pages d'Or/Gouden Gids. T-Service,* operated by the Belgian employment service, also arranges temporary work. There is an office in every city.

Major newspapers also advertise vacancies. These include *Le Soir* (French), *La Libre Belgique* (French), *De Standaard* (Dutch), *Het Nieuwsblad* (Dutch), *De Gazet van Antwerpen* (Dutch) and *Het Laatste Nieuws* (Dutch). On Tuesdays in the summer, *De Standaard* devotes a job column to graduates. Major recruiters often place corporate advertisements in student magazines such as *Knack*, and the French editions, *Le Vif*, *L'Express* and *Intermediaire.*

Directories, including *Move Up*, *Kompass Belgique* and *Top 25000* can provide a useful starting point for a speculative approach to job hunting. Job fairs are held at various times of the year and are advertised nationally as well as regionally; some are held at universities and some at commercial venues.

Applications usually take the form of a two-page typewritten CV with a handwritten covering letter; both preferably in the language of the region to which it is being sent. It is important to remember that appropriate language skills are almost always sought: either Dutch/Flemish or French, depending on the region. French is essential in Wallonia/Brussels and highly desirable in Flanders, while Dutch is necessary in Flanders and useful in Wallonia/Brussels. Brussels is officially bilingual and a knowledge of both languages is usually required.

Belgian governments have introduced a considerable amount of employment legislation. It is interesting that in addition to the normal statutory rights, employees have statutory rights to paid time off for births, marriages, divorces, deaths, religious festivals and study. There is a legal minimum wage for most sectors of employment. All employees automatically receive a pay rise every six months linked to the cost of living. The normal working week is 36–39 hours with 40 hours the maximum normally allowed. Overtime and Sunday working are no longer officially banned, but are only permitted by special arrangements between employers and trade unions. Over 60 per cent of the total work-force in Belgium belong to a union. All companies with more than 50 staff are required to form a works council (*Conseil d'Entreprise/Ondernemingsraad*). The works council deals with any problem related to employment in each organization. Such companies must also have a health and safety committee.

After working one complete calendar year, all employees are entitled to 20 days' paid holiday in the following year. A holiday bonus of 85 per cent of one month's salary may also be paid if there has been a collective agreement for that sector.

The European Commission's head office is based in Brussels and is one of the major employers in Belgium. Temporary contracts with the Commission are advertised through temporary agencies in Brussels. For most jobs with the Commission, certainly those involving administrative or clerical skills, French, German and English language skills are almost always required.

INFORMATION POINTS

Education and training

Confederation Generale des Ensei –
gnats (CGE)
rue de Meridien 22
1030 Brussels

Direction Generale de l'organisation
des Etudes (DGOE)
du Ministére de l'Education de la
Communaute francaise
bd Pacheco 34
1000 Brussels

Ministry of Education for the
French-speaking community
rue de Commerce 68a
1040 Brussels

Pedagogie-recherche-developement
(PIRD)
rue du Viaduc 133
1040 Brussels

Rijksaministratief Centrum
(Ministry of Education for the
Dutch-Speaking community)
CAE Arcadengebouw blok f
6 de Verdieping
1010 Brussels

Vereniging van opleidings – en
vormingsverantwoordelijken (VOV)
Eekhoutstraat 46
8000 Bruges

Vereniging Vlaamse Leerkrachten
(VVL)
Zwijgerstraat 37
2000 Antwerp

Vlaamse Dienst voor
Arbeidsbemiddel en
Beroepsopleiding (VDAB)
Centrum voor Pedagogische
Opleiding en Studie
Viaducstraat 133
1040 Brussels

Employment

Commission of the European
Communities
Recruitment Unit – COM/A/724
rue de la Loi 200
1049 Brussels

Flanders Investment Office (FIOC)
Trierstraat 100
1040 Brussels

Fonds des Accidents du Travail
rue du Trône 100
1050 Brussels

FOREM Head Office
boulevard de l'Empereur 5
1000 Brussels

Ministry of the Brussels Region
rue Royale 2
1000 Brussels

Ministry of Wallonia
av. Prince de Liège 7
5100 Namur

Office National de la Securité Sociale
boulevard de Waterloo 76
1000 Brussels

Office National des Pensions
Tour Midi
1060 Brussels

ORBEM/BGDA Head Office
boulevard Anspach 65
1000 Brussels

Rijksdienst voor Pensioenen
Zuidertoren
1060 Brussels

T-Interim
Lemonnierlaan 129-131
1000 Brussels

VDAB Head Office
Keizerslaan 11
1000 Brussels

European Information Centres

Antwerpen
Kamer van Koophandel en
Nijverheid van Antwerpen
Euro Info Centrum
Markgravestraat 12
2000 Antwerpen

Arlon
CDP – Idelux
Euro Info Centre
avenue Nothomb 8
6700 Arlon

Brussels
Ministerie van de Vlaamse
Gemeenschap
Admn. voor Economie en
Werkgelegenheid
Euro Info Centrum
Markiesstraat 1 – 6e verdieping
1000 Brussels

Chambre de Commerce et
d'Industrie de Bruxelles
Kamar voor Handel en Nijverheid
van Brussel
et/en Fabrimetal
Euro Info Centre Brussels
avenue Louise, 500 Louizalaan
1050 Brussels

Charleroi
Euroguichet Hainaut-Est
Euro Info Centre
avenue Général Michel, 1B
6000 Charleroi

Eupen
(antenne/satellite BE-010)
Schulungs – und Forschungszentrum
SPK
Gospertstrasse, 17
4700 Eupen

Gent
Gewestelijke
Ontwikkelingsmaatscappij
voor Oost-Vlaanderen
Euro Info Centrum
Floraliapaleis, bus 6
9000 Gent

Hasselt
Kamar voor Handel en Nijverheid
van Limburg vzw
Euro Info Centrum Limburg
Kunstlaan 20
3500 Hasselt

Kortrijk
Nationaal Christelijk
Middenstandsverbond Kortrijk
Euro Info Centrum
Lange Steenstraat, 10
8500 Kortrijk

Liège
Institut Provincial des Classes
Moyennes
Euro Info Centre
bd d'Avroy 28-30
4000 Liège

Mons
Bureau d'Etudes Economiques et
Sociales de la Province du Hainaut
Euro Info Centre
rue de Nimy, 50
7000 Mons

Namur
Bureau Economique de la Province
de Namur (BEPN)
Euro Info Centre
avenue Sergent Vrithoff, 2
5000 Namur

Tournai
(antenne/satellite BE-011)
Chambre de Commerce et
d'Industrie du Tournaisis
rue Beyaert, 73-75
7500 Tournai

Zaventem
Kamar voor Handel en Nijverheid
van het Arrondissement
Halle-Vilvoorde en arr. Leuven
Euro Info Centrum Vlaams Brabant
Brucargo Gebouw 706 1 ste verdiep
likaal 7127
1931 Zaventem

Chapter 3

Denmark

KEY FACTS

Surface area	43,075 sq km, 16,631 sq miles
Capital	Copenhagen
Major towns	Aarhus, Odense, Aalborg, Esbjerg, (all ports)
Form of government	liberal democracy
Population	(1990 est) 5,134,000, annual growth rate 0 per cent
Language	Danish (official)
Currency	Kroner
Exports	bacon, dairy produce, eggs, fish, mink pelts, car and aircraft parts, electrical equipment, textiles, chemicals
Vocational educational institutions	trade/vocational trade school
Awarding organizations	Apprenticeship Committee or Trade Committee
Grants	means-tested scholarships are available to maintain students in further and higher education and state guaranteed bank loans are a second option. Many students combine study with paid employment

Vocational qualifications	training certificate
Trends/developments	in 1992 new initiatives and measures to make it easier for adults to take a vocational training course were introduced. They have been set up for two reasons to combat long-term unemployment and to bridge the skills gap

EDUCATION SYSTEM

Responsibility for education in Denmark is shared between the central state authorities, counties, municipalities and private institutions under the overall supervision of the Ministry of Education. Within national guidelines, local councils have considerable autonomy in deciding the system in their schools. No fees are payable in public schools attended by over 90 per cent of pupils.

Compulsory education is from 7 to 16. All services for children under this age are the responsibility of the Ministry of Social Affairs and local authority social welfare departments, with two exceptions – pre-primary schooling and school-based outside school hours care, which are the responsibility of education departments in most local authorities. Services have a dual care and education function; the education function is seen in broad terms of enhancing a child's overall development. In the 3–6 age group, all 5- and 6-year-olds go to pre-primary schooling, which is available for three hours a day in primary schools.

Compulsory education

Since 1976 Denmark has had a two-tier system of compulsory education of nine years, from age 7 to 16 (in a *folkeskole*), followed by a voluntary tenth year, or alternatively a transfer at age 15 to the *gymnasium* (grammar school) or upper secondary school.

The school year begins in the second week in August and comprises 200 days and excludes weekends. The school day broadly covers 8am until 2 or 3pm, without a long lunch break, but the number of weekly periods range from 15 to 23, for 7- to 8-year-olds, up to 24 to 34 for grades 8, 9 and 10. The class size cannot exceed 28; there is no minimum size.

The system is comprehensive, as the class remains together for most subjects, but from the 8th grade can divide into basic and advanced levels for mathematics, English and German, and from the 9th grade for physics and chemistry. The teacher of Danish is usually the 'home room' teacher, responsible also for pastoral care and often remaining with the class for the whole nine compulsory years. Grades 1 and 2 have two teachers but as more subjects feature, more staff are involved. Four subjects are taught every year, namely Danish (including the very similar Norwegian and Swedish), mathematics, physical training and religious education. Other subjects must feature in certain years, as follows: grades 1 to 5, art and music; grades 4, 5 and 6, needlework, woodwork and domestic science respectively (for both sexes); grades 3 to 9, history; 3 to 7, geography and biology; 8 and 9, contemporary studies and 5 to 9, English and physics. German must be offered in grades 7 to 9. A weekly class discussion period is timetabled, to plan trips and also for (compulsory) instruction in road safety, and health and sex education. In grades 8 to 10 various vocational (eg, typing, metalwork, clerical duties, woodwork) or artistic (eg, drama, dance, pottery, photography) options can be offered and also, for short periods, employer-based work experience.

Progress is reported to pupils and parents at least twice a year, but specific marks or grades are not given until the seventh grade. Voluntary exams can be taken in the eighth, ninth and tenth grade for the leaving examinations of the *folkeskole* (primary and lower secondary school).

Special education

Integration is the favoured method of educational support for children with special needs in Denmark. As far as possible, provision is made for all children and young people with motor, sensory and learning disabilities within the main school system. An educational psychologist must be attached to every school.

Upper secondary school

Upper secondary school courses last for three years. Entry requires German, plus the leaving certificate in Danish and mathematics, plus either English, German and Latin, or physics and chemistry, and also the school's recommendation to attend upper secondary school. The first year divides into either the languages or the maths-science stream, which subdivides further in the second and third year into four and three streams respectively, namely modern languages, music, social science and classics, and maths/physics, natural science, social science. The course ends with a state controlled examination, one route for entry to higher education.

In most cases, this involves the *studentereksamen* (upper secondary school-leaving examination). However, possession of the *studentereksamen* does not mean automatic acceptance into a higher education institution because almost all higher education courses are restricted by *numerus clausus*: a quotient which is laid down each year for the various courses, whereby the average marks for admission to the various disciplines are set. Therefore, for many applicants, admission is on the basis of their average marks in the *studentereksamen.*

Administration

Universities and other colleges are mainly run by the state, while upper secondary schools and higher preparatory courses (HF) are managed by the 14 counties.

The National Parliament legislates the overall aims, defining the general framework of education. The Ministry of Education issues various mandatory decrees as well as optional guidelines. The Ministry controls final examination practices and procedures, and lays down minimum standards for school buildings. Within this framework the education committees of locally elected councils have considerable autonomy, especially for compulsory education; managing schools in conjunction with individual school boards, which decide jointly the number of lessons, curricula, educational equipment and teaching methods. Each school must also have a parents council, to ensure pupil attendance and cooperation between the school and home. The same council is also allowed to comment on the timetable and textbooks, and in many cases it has considerable influence to alter educational practices.

Finance

Public expenditure on education accounts for an average of 7.7 per cent of GNP per year. In addition the Ministry of Social Affairs supports day nurseries and kindergartens.

Education is mainly free; municipalities receive block grants and allocate funds to schools. The money is not earmarked by the state, so there is quite considerable autonomy for local authorities. The private sector is responsible for a minority of pupils (some 8 per cent) and certain colleges, eg, child welfare teacher training courses, engineering colleges, and most teacher training colleges, are mainly independent institutions. Agricultural schools and continuation schools are also private. The private sector receives large state subsidies, about half for folk high schools, and charges fees, except in teacher training colleges.

Means-tested scholarships and grants are available to maintain students in further and higher education and state guaranteed bank loans are another option. Many students combine study with paid employment, a far higher proportion, in fact, than in most other EC countries.

VOCATIONAL EDUCATION SYSTEM

Post-compulsory education

One in five pupils leave the education system without further education or training, which represents one of the lowest leaving rates in the EC. In Denmark vocational education and training is provided in sandwich-type courses in which theoretical education at a vocational school alternates with practical training in a business environment. At the tenth grade of secondary education, pupils can choose between a three-year upper secondary school course, apprenticeship (practical training in a firm alternating with theoretical/commercial school), or vocational training (a basic year with theoretical education at a technical/commercial school followed by two years' practical training in a firm).

The basic principle of the Danish system of vocational training is the dual system, based on alternating periods of school education and on-the-job training. The dual system (EFG) as operated in Denmark is similar to the old UK system of part-time day or block release to college combined with practical on-the-job work experience. Running parallel to the EFG are the well established apprentice training courses. As well as leading directly to employment, EFG and apprentice training courses qualify students for admission to certain non-academic higher education courses, or, in combination with an entrance exam, to engineering courses at *teknika* (engineering colleges).

A process is underway in Denmark to reorganize basic vocational training which is expected to alter the capacity of the training system to keep abreast of developments and respond to the challenges posed by technological and social changes. Two new laws were passed in Spring 1989, one concerning the management of vocational colleges, technical schools and business schools (Statute No 210 of 5 April 1989), and the other regulating the actual structure of vocational training and the advisory and management committees and boards concerned (Statute No 211 of 5 April 1989). These measures came into force on 1 January 1991. The new legislation has amalgamated the two hitherto competing forms of apprentice training (ie, master training according to the Apprentice Act of 1956 and the EFG apprentice training according to the EFG of 1977) in a new formula that incorporates principles from both the previous routes. The common core of the establishment and completion of a course of industrial training remains the setting up of a training contract between the individual young person and the firm. Training plans, or apprenticeship contracts, prescribe rights and obligations on employers and on employees (trainees). The rules for training contracts are drawn up by the various trade committees, parity bodies with equal representation of employers' organizations and the trade unions.

Industrial boards must authorize the firm to enter into training contracts and are also responsible for drafting the rules for the firm's side of the training within the commercial and industrial training programmes. These formal training regulations have to be formally authorized by the Minister of Education.

The new vocational training reform stipulates that the industrial boards must maintain a division and balance between basic education, general training, special training and the specific trade in order to provide a certain breadth or solidarity between the related trades and gradual specialization. The reforms lay considerable emphasis on the importance of practical in-firm training, and on the crucial role of interaction between training by firms and school teaching.

Technical schools

Technical schools provide various full-time vocational courses of two to four years in a range of occupational areas, for example, laboratory technicians, building technicians, catering, agriculture, etc. Commercial schools provide both one-year courses leading to a certificate, and two-year diplomas, which in certain subjects are acceptable admission qualifications for HE entry.

Apprentices

Each apprentice must have completed nine years of compulsory education before entering a contract with an employer. Apprenticeships last for two to four years depending on the trade and the final job aim, and combine employer-based training with formalized education at a technical or commercial school. Wages are paid and tuition is free. Administration of apprenticeship training in Denmark is the responsibility of the Department of Education through its twin Directorates of Youth Education and Vocational Training. This latter Directorate cooperates with employers and employees through joint trade boards which report through a national apprenticeship board.

A recent alternative to apprenticeships which has been in existence since 1 January 1991 is basic vocational training in a school-like environment, without a contract and without employer involvement until the second year. In other words, it has introduced a means of replacing practical work experience within companies by a totally school-based vocational course. The first year involves full-time technical school study in one of nine sectors; followed by up to three years' combined paid work experience and study. This alternative was introduced primarily because a recurring problem since the 1970s has been the shortage of apprenticeships and training places. As a stop-gap measure, this new method represents an opportunity for young people to complete their training by extending schooling. The government has appointed a committee to examine the scheme and to evaluate the implications for the Danish vocational education and training system.

Higher education

Some 0.1 million students enrol annually in one of two types of institution: universities or specialized institutions. University courses take four to seven years, and other colleges three to five years, depending on the subject(s) and coverage.

In principle, those holding the upper secondary school leaving examination (*studentereksamen*), the higher preparatory examination (HF) or the higher commercial examination (HH) are entitled to enter higher education. Since 1977, however, quotas have been set on the number of admissions into each institution and each subject department.

Successful completion of an academic higher education course leads to the acquisition of an examination certificate (*eksamenbevis*) and/or a degree (*grad*) or title (*titel*). First degrees are called *kandidateksamen* and are by far the most common university qualification.

Universities and institutions of higher education in Denmark

There are five universities in Denmark. The largest and oldest is the University of Copenhagen, which was established in 1479. Aarhus University was established in 1928. The three most recent universities are from the 1960s and 1970s; they are located in Odense, Roskilde and Aalborg.

Besides the universities, a number of specialized institutions offer education at academic level in a number of subjects, for example, engineering, dental sciences, veterinary and agricultural sciences, pharmacy, business studies and modern languages and educational studies.

Most students admitted to higher education have passed the examination for the General Certificate of Education, A-level (*studentereksamen*), but other examinations also qualify for admission. Mature students without formal qualifications who can nevertheless demonstrate an ability to undertake a higher education course are given ample consideration during selection procedures.

Most institutions offer degrees at Bachelor's as well as Master's level. A Danish Master's degree generally requires five years of study and as a rule ends with a thesis. The structure of studies varies with institutions and subject areas, but in recent years official policy has been to locate a Bachelor's-level degree within all disciplines after three years of study have been undertaken successfully.

The principles of governance at universities and institutions of higher education are regulated by an Act of Parliament passed in 1970. Every institution is administered by a vice-chancellor (*rektor*), in collaboration with a number of collegiate bodies and committees. In these bodies students and technical staff have some representation, but the teaching staff generally hold the majority.

Teacher training

Lower secondary, pre-school and primary teacher training is organized in specific colleges, preparing students to teach at a specific level or in a particular subject area, such as home economics, woodcraft or general science. Universities and university colleges provide courses for those aiming at upper secondary school teaching. Courses last for three to four years and are mainly theoretical, but with some practical work experience included. The latter may be undertaken in a Danish school, or if a 'home' placement cannot be arranged, a student can arrange for his or her placement to be in another EC country.

Adult Education

A wide range of provision exists in general, vocational and leisure education for adults. Regular education for 14–18-year-olds can be supplemented in continuation (10 month residential vocational), and youth schools (all types of provision outside school hours); the latter include youth clubs and are attended by 60 per cent of the age group. Short vocational courses of two to three weeks are available for those aged 18 or over, leading to a certificate. A two-year full-time course leads to the Higher Preparatory Examination for adults to qualify for HE entrance, and can also be taken in stages by part-time study.

Evening classes, weekend residential courses and distance learning courses are all well established in Denmark. Most educational courses are organized by local authorities or private sponsors, including the *Workers Education Association* and the *Popular Education Association*.

Since 1989 a scheme has been in operation whereby adults without a vocational training background may obtain leave from their workplace in order to receive education/training. Originally this was intended as a temporary measure but due to its popularity it has now been made permanent. The scheme is administered by the Ministry of Cultural Affairs. Under the scheme it is possible to obtain leave from the workplace for one to 16 weeks within a two-year period. In order to obtain such leave the person concerned must satisfy the following conditions. He or she must:

- be between 25 and 60 years of age;
- be economically active, ie, working as an employee or self-employed person;

- have only a basic education background and no or only poor vocational skills;
- have been working for his or her present employer for at least 26 consecutive weeks.

It is possible to combine this scheme with another called the 'job offer scheme' so that the enterprise takes on a long-term unemployed person with a wage subsidy while the employee is on leave for education/training purposes. This way, current employees benefit through greater access to vocational training, and unemployed persons benefit through access to work experience. The job offer scheme is administered by the Public Employment Service.

Vocational training with an international dimension

There are approximately 85 vocational education and training courses in Denmark, which in many subject areas is not sufficient to meet demand. For some years, the lack of training places within enterprises in Denmark has been a growing problem. At the same time, training places are often vacant in other Member States. In 1992, legislative proposals were in the pipeline to enable young people to take part of their practical training in other countries within the EC or the EFTA areas. This new move will facilitate vocational courses with an international dimension. It is intended that the trainees will be paid an extra amount of money to cover travel expenses and boarding costs. The subsidy will be paid by the AER (Employers' reimbursement for trainees wages). About 1000 young people are expected to use this opportunity each year.

In 1991, the social partners in cooperation with the Danish Ministries of Labour and Education founded an organization called ACIU, (the Danish Centre for International Training Programmes). The work of the centre is funded by the founding organizations, the two Ministries and the EC. The aim of the ACIU is to strengthen the internationalization of Danish training and education. ACIU deals with training and education for working life, that is vocational training, company training and continued education related to work. As such, ACIU has a close connection with the Danish labour market.

ECONOMIC FEATURES

Denmark is the smallest but most densely populated country in northern Europe, and is believed to be the oldest kingdom in the world. It consists of the low-lying Jutland peninsula and about 500 islands, 90 of which are inhabited. The Jutland peninsula is linked to the rest of Europe by the border with Germany.

Denmark is generally regarded as an agricultural country, but there have been dramatic changes in recent years and today only some 7 per cent of the population is employed in agriculture and forestry. It has a large fishing and merchant fleet and there are strong international trading links. Because of the high cost of importing coal and oil, the Danes are developing their own exploration of North Sea oil and gas. In addition, they are pioneers in non-polluting energy sources, notably the huge wind generators which are found in windmill parks set up throughout the country.

About 10 per cent of the country is covered by woodland, including commercial forests. Shipping and furniture manufacturing feature high on the economic agenda. In fact, today the leading sector of the economy is manufacturing. Other products include silverware, processed food, dairy products, chemical and engineering goods.

Industrial zones

In June 1990, the *folketing* decided that it should be possible to establish industrial zones in three of the 14 Danish counties, namely Northern Jutland, Storstrom and Bornholm. Included in the plan was a decision to establish up to 10 industrial zones in the three counties, each covering an area of about 50 hectares.

The aim of this new labour market policy is to create new jobs in the regions in Denmark which have the most urgent need for employment growth. An industrial zone is a geographical area within which enterprises are offered special favourable conditions with a view to strengthening development in trade and industry and in employment within the area concerned.

The special favourable conditions are: quick procedures for approval of applications to set up new enterprises; and the possibility of obtaining exemption from certain legislative rules such as holiday legislation, working environment legislation and other labour law rules.

With regard to the possibility of obtaining exemption from labour law legislation, the aim is not to abolish this legislation in the industrial zones, but to comply with wishes expressed by enterprises and their employees for a more flexible and less bureaucratic set of rules. As a positive side-effect, perusal of applications for exemption will also show whether and in which areas the rules concerned have unintended effects and hamper the growth potential of enterprises. Exemptions will not be granted from rules originating from EC directives or ILO conventions. The industrial zones will be set up following negotiations between the Minister of Industry and the individual municipalities.

New rules on leave from the labour market

As part of the so-called 'activation package' adopted by the *folketing* in June 1992, new schemes concerning leave from the labour market have been introduced and are outlined below.

Parental leave
Under this temporary scheme (operative from 1 July 1992 until 1 January 1994), parents with children under the age of 9 may now be given paid leave in order to take care of them, provided that a substitute is recruited. The aim of this scheme is twofold: first, to give more unemployed persons better opportunities for job training through job rotation and, second, to help families with small children. The scheme applies to both the public and private sectors.

In order to obtain leave, the employee must satisfy the conditions for obtaining unemployment benefit and the same applies to the unemployed substitute who must be recruited for at least the same number of working hours.

The period of leave is for 13 to 36 consecutive weeks. If the child is under the age of 3, the use of public child care facilities during the period of parental leave will not be permitted. If the child is between 3 and 8 years of age, public child care facilities may be used on a half-day basis.

The employee on parental leave receives 80 per cent of the maximum rate of unemployment benefit, ie DKr 2040 per week. The employer may choose to pay the full wage during the period of leave. The substitute is paid the full wage fixed by collective agreement for the type of work concerned. The unemployment insurance fund pays the allowance to the person on leave or to the employer if he or she pays the full wage to the employee.

An employee who wishes to take parental leave must reach an agreement with the employer specifying the duration of the leave and the conditions for returning to the job. A special form obtainable from the Public Employment Service must be completed and the Public Employment Service may also assist the employer in finding a substitute.

This parental leave scheme is very liberal and flexible. For instance, it is possible to combine parental leave with maternity leave. Both parents may take leave at the same time and there is no limit to the number of periods of leave.

Leave for training purposes
This scheme makes it possible to obtain leave for educational/training purposes for four to 36 consecutive weeks provided that the employer recruits an unemployed person as a substitute.

The aim of the scheme is two-fold: to make it possible for people in employment to acquire new skills and qualifications and to bring unemployed persons back into employment. The scheme is intended for both full-time and part-time employed persons who are members of an unemployment insurance fund. It is a condition for obtaining leave with financial remuneration that the persons concerned have had a stable position in the labour market and that they have been working for their present employer for at least one year.

The scheme applies to both the public and private sectors and is administered by the public Employment Service. The provisions as regards financial remuneration to the person taking leave for educational/training purposes and the wage paid to the substitute are the same as those described above applying to parental leave. The administrative procedures are also the same.

Training and job rotation

The aim of this scheme is to promote job rotation in the private sector in order to improve employment opportunities for the unemployed and to improve the general level of skills of the labour force. The right to be absent from work may be granted for four to 36 consecutive weeks provided that the employer recruits a substitute. The scheme is linked with the Act on Educational Support to Adults (the so-called VUS – *voksenuddannelsesstotte*) and is administered by the Ministry for Cultural Affairs.

The employee receives his or her normal full wage while undergoing education/training in the absence of any other agreement between the employer and the employee. The substitute is paid the normal contractual wage within the sector concerned. The Ministry of Cultural Affairs reimburses the employer. The amount of this reimbursement corresponds to the maximum level of unemployment benefit.

FINDING EMPLOYMENT

EC nationals have the right to live and work in Denmark without a work permit. A full EC passport is essential, and a visitor's passport or excursion document is not sufficient. EC nationals are free to enter Denmark for up to three months to look for work or to set up in business. If a stay of over three months is intended, a residence permit (*opholdstilladelse*) is required. In order to obtain an *opholdstilladelse* it is necessary to:

- have suitable accomodation;
- have a job which meets government guidelines on hours and salary;
- be a member of an unemployment fund (unemployment funds are administered by trade unions). Unemployment benefit levels are approximately 90 per cent of previous earnings. It is possible to

become a member of a special non-union unemployment fund called *A-Kasse*.

Visitors who satisfy these three requirements can obtain an *opholdstilladelse* from local police stations in Denmark.

A personal code certificate number (*personnummer*) and social security certificate (*sygesikringsbevis*) are also required by anyone who stays in Denmark on more than a tourist basis. These are required for all dealings with Danish authorities. A *personnummer* is issued by the civil register authorities (*Folkeregisteret*). A *sygesikringsbevis* is required for access to the public hospital service.

EC nationals working in Denmark have the same rights as Danish nationals with regard to pay, working conditions, access to housing, vocational training and education, social security and trade union membership. EC nationals have free access to the services of the Danish employment service. Danish job centres are called *Arbejdformidling* (AF). The address of the nearest AF office can be found in telephone directories (*navnebogens*) or the Danish equivalent of the Yellow Pages, *de Gule Sider*. Private employment agencies are called *vikarbureauer* and are listed under that heading in *De Gule Sider*.

Newspapers also advertise vacancies. The major newspapers in Denmark include *Politiken*, *Berlingske Tidende* (the Sunday issue has the largest jobs section in the Danish press), *Jyllands-Posten*, *Ekstrabladet*, *Aktuelt* and *BT*. For jobs in Jutland, *Morgenavisen Jyllandsposten* is the most useful newspaper. As well as newspapers, journals may be useful for jobhunting in some specialist areas, for example, *Ingenioren* for engineering, *DJOF-bladet* for economics and law, and *Det Dansk Bogmarked* for publishing and printing.

Applications should be written in Danish. CVs and covering letters should be accompanied by photocopies of degree certificates and other qualifications. Details about past work experience and qualifications are important to include, but extra-curricular details such as interests and hobbies less so. References do not need to be supplied by jobseekers as they are not usually required by employers.

Most regulations concerning employment issues in Denmark are based on national collective agreements between employers and trade unions rather than on government legislation. Over 80 per cent of employees belong to a union. Any business with over 35 employees must have an employer–employee cooperation committee. Minimum wages for each sector are negotiated every six months between employee and employer organizations. The normal working week is between 37 and 39 hours and is set by collective agreements. A minimum of five weeks' annual leave plus 13 days' public holidays is established by law. All wage earners are entitled to holiday pay (*feriepenge*). A little over 12 per cent of each employee's wages earned during the previous year is paid by the employer to the national holiday fund (*FerieGiro*). Employers must ensure that each employee receives a holiday fund card (*feriegiro Kort*) which shows entitlement to holiday pay. This card can be cashed at any post office in Denmark.

INFORMATION POINTS

Education and training

Danish Centre for International
Training Programmes (ACIU)
Guldborgvej 25
2000 Frederiksberg

Danmarks Teknologiske Institut
Att. Birthe Hedegaard
Gregersensvej
2630 Tastrup

Statens Erhervspaedagogiske
Laereruddannelse
Att. John Houman Sorensen
Rigensgade 13
1316 Copenhagen

The Royal Danish School of
Educational Studies for Teachers
and Technical and Commercial
Colleges (SEL)
13 Rigensgade
1316 Copenhagen

Undervisningsministeriet
(Danish Ministry of Education
international relations)
Internationale Kontor
Frederiksholm Kanal 25D
1220 Copenhagen

Employment

Arbejdsmarkedsstyrelsen
(Head office of the Danish
employment service)
Adelgade 13
1304 Copenhagen

British Council
Montergade 1
1116 Copenhagen

British Embassy
Kastelsvej 36
2100 Copenhagen

Det Danske Handelskammer
(Danish Chamber of Commerce)
Borsen
1217 Copenhagen

FerieGiro (national holiday fund)
Arbejdsmarkedets Feriefond
Kongens Vaenge
3400 Hillerod

Ferielovkontoret
(Holiday fund)
Landskronagade 33-35
2100 Copenhagen

Folkeregisteret (civil register
authority)
Dahlerupsgade 6
1640 Copenhagen

Skatteministeriet (Ministry of taxes)
Slothsholmsgade 12
1216 Copenhagen

Undervisningsministeriet
(Danish Ministry of Education
international relations)
Frederiksholm Kanal 25D
1220 Copenhagen

Youth Information Kobenhavn/'Use It'
Rådhusstræde 13
1446 Copenhagen

European Information Centres

Aabenraa
Sonderjyllands Erhvervsråd
Euro Info Centre
Kirkeplads 4
6200 Aabenraa

Århus
EF-Rådgivningskontoret
Regionskontoret Århus
Amts-Kommune
Euro Info Centre
Haslegaardsvænget 18–20
8210 Århus

Copenhagen
Dansk Teknisk Oplysningstjeneste
Euro Info Centre
Rygaards Alle 131 A
Postbox 1992
2820 Copenhagen

Det Danske Handelskammer
Euro Info Centre
Borsen
1217 Copenhagen

Herning
Herning Erhvervsråd
Euro Info Centre
Lykkesvej 18
7400 Herning

Odense
EF-Rådgivningskontoret for Fyn
Euro Info Centre
Norregade 51
5000 Odense

Viborg
Håndvoerksrådet
Euro Info Centre
Li. Sct. Hans Gade 20
8800 Viborg

Vordingborg
Storstroms Erhvervscenter
Euro Info Centre
Marianbergvej 80
4760 Vordingborg

Chapter 4

France

KEY FACTS

Surface area	(including Corsica) 543,965 sq km, 210,026 sq miles
Capital	Paris
Major towns	Lyons, Lille, Bordeaux, Toulouse, Nantes, Strasbourg; ports Marseilles, Nice, Le Havre
Form of government	liberal democracy
Population	(1990 est) 56,184,000, annual growth rate 0.3 per cent
Language	French (regional dialects include Breton, Catalan, Provencal)
Currency	French franc
Exports	fruit (especially apples), wine, cheese, automobiles, aircraft, chemicals, jewellery, silk, lace; tourism is very important
Vocational educational institutions	vocational schools; apprentice training centres; adult vocational training centres
Awarding organizations	Ministry of National Education; Ministry of Labour, Employment and Training

Grants	student support is available in the form of grants and scholarships
Vocational qualifications	vocational training certificate and diplomas
Trends/developments	trend towards increased investment by enterprises in the vocational training and development of their employees, and increased provision for training outside working time, known generally as co-investment training

EDUCATION SYSTEM

The state education system is administered by the Ministry of National Education, which exerts more control than elsewhere in Europe. National criteria standardize administration, finance and curricula; teaching staff and school assistants are state officials and the state has the monopoly over the award of diplomas. Tuition is free in public educational establishments; in universities and many *grandes écoles* nominal fees are levied. Grants or scholarships are available in cases where financial need can be proven. Public education is secular, and religious education is not included in school curricula. Private educational institutions also exist, which are organized and maintained by private citizens, associations, professional bodies and religious organizations, usually with some degree of help from the state in return for some control over standards and staffing. For instance heavily subsidized Catholic schools which charge low fees to many people provide an alternative to the state provision which is attractive to many parents in urban areas and is the dominant form of education provision in some regions such as Brittany.

Education is compulsory between the ages of 6 and 16 but nursery or pre-school education is provided for children between 2 and 5 years either in separate nursery schools or in infant departments of primary schools. Pre-primary schools (*écoles maternelles*) cater for 2- to 5-year-olds, and although attendance is voluntary, local authorities are required by law to provide pre-primary education. These schools are open from 8.30 to 16.30 and most provide meals and supervision during the two-hour lunch break. Although pre-primary schooling is widely available, there are large local variations in other services, especially for children under 3. Large towns have the best supply of services, rural areas least; for example, nearly half the nursery places available in France are in the Ile-de-France area, in and around Paris.

Compulsory education

Compulsory education lasts for ten years, from 6 to 16. The school year runs from mid-September to the end of June. The school day is long, followed by compulsory homework at the secondary level. Most schools are closed on Wednesdays and open on Saturday mornings, although since the early 1980s local authorities have the power to alter this arrangement.

Primary education

Undertaken in primary schools (*écoles elementaires*), primary education starts at age 6, exceptionally 5, and is divided into three cycles. The structure is flexible with provision for year skipping and extra coaching to avoid repetition, which none the less is commonplace; by the beginning of secondary school, only about half the children are the normal age for the class. The 27-hour school week is occupied with a curriculum based on the 3Rs which is common to all children.

Secondary education

Secondary education is divided into two cycles; the first cycle, which consists of two stages, falls within compulsory education and is taught mainly in *collèges* (comprehensive schools) from completion of primary education to age 15. The first two years are unstreamed, and referred to as the 'observation stage', with a common core curriculum of 21 hours a week for all pupils, consisting of the traditional subjects, a foreign language, and some more modern subjects, eg, experimental science, and technical education. For every subject there is a precise national programme, defining the criteria and content. In addition all children have three hours a week of sport. Extra classes in French, mathematics and a foreign language, on a remedial or more academic basis, and optional sporting and/or artistic activities, occupy the remaining time. The normal class size is 24, the maximum is 30. Pupils then move on to the two-year orientation stage which consists of either general education with the same core curriculum as the first stage with extra obligatory and voluntary classes, leading on satisfactory completion to the awarding on a continuous assessment basis by the *collège*, of a certificate, the *brevet d'études du premier cycle* (BEP); or classes with a vocational bias, on transfer to a vocational *lycée* (*lycée d'enseignement professionel* [LEP]), in which the pupil may start on a three-year course leading to a craft qualification, the *certificat d'Aptitude Professionelle* (CAP) in one of over 300 subjects. About 12 per cent of 14-year-olds take this option. For those who remain at the *collège*, the second cycle begins at age 15-plus. Pupils are guided by counselling into that part of it most suited to their aptitudes and ability.

Special education

Special education establishments in France are governed by the Ministry of Education, Health or Social Affairs, depending on the type of disability. Although integration is favoured, special schools and units are also provided for children with motor, sensory and learning disabilities. In addition, there are special residential schools for children too severely afflicted to attend ordinary schools.

French education and training levels

Level V1: Staff occupying posts not requiring any training beyond the end of compulsory schooling.
Level Va: Staff occupying posts requiring a short period of training of a maximum of one year.
Level V: Staff occupying posts normally requiring a qualification, equivalent to a *brevet d'études professionelles* (BEP) or a *certificat d'aptitude professionelle* (CAP) – craft level.
Level 1V: Staff occupying supervisory posts or with a qualification equivalent to a technical or vocational baccalaureat or technician's diploma.
Level 111: Staff occupying posts requiring a level of training of *brevet de technicien superieur*; a diploma from one of the *instituts universitaires de technologies,* or a diploma obtained at the end of the first cycle (two years) of higher education.
Level 1 and 11: Staff occupying posts normally requiring a level of training of a least a degree or a qualification from an *école d'ingenieurs*.

Administration

Central control of finance, curricula, administration and the award of degrees and diplomas is exerted by the Ministry through 28 *Académies*, each headed by a *rector*, assisted by a permanent administration, an *inspectorate* and regional advisory councils. At the departmental level (two to six per academy), the *inspecteur d'académie* directs the educational services under the authority of the *rector*. There is a central *inspectorate*, dealing with national matters, and local *inspectorates* who handle matters at both department and academy level. The *inspecteur d'académie* has delegated powers of financial control and wide powers of inspection. The appraisal of individual teachers is also the role of the *inspectorate*.

National non-government agencies which advise on educational technology, the curriculum, teaching methods, teacher training, administration and the professions also exist in France. The *Centre National de la Recherche Scientifique* (CNRS) can, for example, be compared with UK research councils. Although it maintains its own institutes, it is also involved in sponsoring, advising and funding research in all branches of science and technology.

Finance

All children between the ages of 6 and 16 residing in France are entitled to free education in state schools. The main state system of education is financed primarily by central government, with smaller contributions from local public administration, industry and parents. Teachers and officials are state employees and their salaries constitute the largest part of the budget. Although tuition in the state school system is free, parents of pupils in some types of school are obliged to pay for textbooks. About 10 per cent of the total central government schools budget goes on aid to private schools. By far the largest proportion of this aid goes on teachers' salaries.

Vocational further education is partly funded by industry through the *taxe d'apprentissage*, in recognition of the service provided by the state in this area.

Fees in the public sector of higher education are only nominal. Student support is available in the form of grants and scholarships. These are lower than in the UK, but more French students live at home and certain facilities are subsidized by the government.

VOCATIONAL EDUCATION SYSTEM

Post-compulsory education

The second cycle of secondary education is, for the most part, in post-compulsory education. Pupils wishing to continue in full-time education can do so by taking either a short-term or a long-term course.

About 25 per cent of pupils aged 15-plus join a vocational *lycée* for the two-year short course leading to a craft qualification: the CAP or the BEP. Both the CAP and the less narrowly specialized BEP are recognized for entry to jobs in industry and commerce. Alternatively, holders could choose to embark on the *baccalauréat professionel* which was created in 1990 as a direct qualification for employment. It includes many different sections covering all industrial and service sector specialisms. It is intended for students of the short technical programme who hold a BEP or a CAP, and is also open to secondary school students who have completed the first year of the *baccalauréat technologique*.

Long courses are for three years, most leading to the *baccalauréat* which is an external multi-subject examination allowing automatic entry to higher education and qualifying for some professions. The *baccalauréat* is a national diploma and represents successful completion of secondary studies, either general, technical or vocational, and marks the end of 12 years of education. They are taken in *lycées*, some of which are designated *lycées d'enseignement technique* (technical *lycées*). The aim of the *lycées* is to provide grounding in '*culture générale*' (and career preparation in technical *lycées*). The first year is basically unstreamed with eight basic subjects (French, history, geography-civics, one modern language, mathematics, physical sciences, natural sciences and physical training). After this fairly broad start, there is greater specialization in the second and third years in preparation for the chosen *baccalauréat*. There are five general *baccalauréats* with eight options and three technical, or vocational, with 18 options. French and physical education are compulsory to all series; philosophy, history or geography and a modern language to most. A typical candidate is subject to written and oral examinations lasting 18 hours in seven subjects. To pass the exam, students must average 10/20 (subjects are weighted in averaging to reflect their importance); 7/20 or below is an outright fail, but those who fail with 8 or 9/20 can proceed to a second stage examination which gives a chance to improve their mark. This consists of oral examinations in two subjects. If the mark is still 8 or 9, the *certificat de fin d'études* is awarded. The pass rate is about 66 per cent. The syllabuses and timetable are set by the Ministry, but setting (within a certain format) and marking of the examination is the responsibility of the *académie* (the local administrative unit: there are 28 *académies*). The *baccalauréat* officially constitutes the first higher education diploma. Some technical *lycée* students proceed to the more narrowly vocational *Brevet de Technicien*, rather than the *baccalauréat*. This three-year course has 57 varieties, grouped in 12 broad types (eg, building, textile, art, engineering, science).

Transition from school to work

Preparation for adulthood is encouraged by various activities within and outside the school day, organized by pupils with adults cooperating to make the school or college a real educational community. Two related kinds of projects can be identified: first, multidisciplinary activities linking classwork, and second, those meeting pupils' educational and cultural needs, such as youth clubs or assistance for pupils with learning difficulties.

School leavers may enter two-year apprenticeships, with part-time attendance at an apprentice training centre. Seventeen-year-olds may sign a contract of *emploi-formation* of at least six months, which guarantees some training either with the employer or at an outside training centre.

Forty per cent of France's unemployed are in the 16–25 age group. There are various measures to occupy the young unemployed, notably the national '16 to 18 plan', as well as subsidized jobs and training initiatives, not to mention national service which occupies up to 300,000 young men at any one time. In addition, there are two schemes offering incentives to employers to take on young people; and six schemes to provide young unemployed with basic vocational training, mostly involving industrial attachment for various periods. Industrial observation and attachment is prevalent in vocational courses in France. Careers guidance is highly developed, with a three-tier structure of advisers in institutions, regional centres and a national information service which issues pamphlets and handbooks.

In contrast to most countries, there is little criticism by employers of basic standards, although there is some dissatisfaction with the quality of crafts trainees trained on the 14-plus vocational *lycée* course. Employers appear to prefer apprenticeships. Apparently there is a shortage of top level technicians.

New legislation on vocational training and employment

Law 91-1405 of 31 December 1991 on vocational training and employment came into force in Spring 1992. It amends and supplements various measures of the French labour code. Some of the law comprises measures which relate to vocational training, including:

- modification of the regulations on the financing of recurrent training in companies;
- the creation of orientation contracts for under-23-year-olds.

The law also includes employment measures, such as:

- exemptions from employers' social security contributions for the recruitment of young persons aged between 18 and 25 years who have no qualifications;
- the extension of forms of assistance which have already been decreed such as the Return to Work Contract, and assistance for hiring a household's first wage earner.

Vocational training and integration

In the field of vocational training and integration, the most important measures of the new law are as follows:

- employer participation in recurrent training in enterprises with fewer than 10 employees and the introduction of a compulsory contribution corresponding to at least 0.15 per cent of the salaries paid during the year concerned. This payment must be made before 1 March of the year following the year for which the participation is due;
- financing in enterprises with 10 or more employees. The minimum contribution is brought to 1.4 per cent of the wage bill as of 1 January 1992, ie, for the salaries paid during the year 1992 (1.2 per cent up until now). As of 1 January 1993, the rate was increased to 1.5 per cent. As of the same date, the proportion of financing for the Individual Training Leave (*Conge Individual de Formation* – CIF) will increase from 0.15 per cent to 0.2 per cent of the wage bill;
- a new 'orientation contract' replaces the 'Initiation into working life traineeships'. As opposed to the previous measure, this involves a real fixed-term contract (three to six months), non-renewable, available for under-23-year olds (certain under-26-year-olds are also eligable according to conditions laid down by decree), who have at the most completed the second cycle of secondary education. Recruitment on the basis of an orientation contract will be accompanied by exemption from employers' social security contributions due for insurance, occupational accidents and family benefits. Those holding such a contract will receive a salary which will be fixed as a percentage of the statutory minimum wage (SMIC);
- the possibility to draw up an assessment of ability for certain wage earners with their consent. The aim is to enable an analysis to be made of their professional and personal skills so as to define a vocational project. Persons who have worked as wage earners for at least five years, which are not necessarily consecutive (but 12 months of which must be for the present employer), will be eligible for training leave corresponding to a maximum of 24 hours of working time.

Broader access to qualifications

The system of 'individualized training credit' (*Credit de Formation individualise* – CFI) has been on offer to young people aged between 16 and 25 years since September 1989. On 28 March 1990, it was made accessible to all wage earners by draft agreement, and to adult jobseekers. This represents the last step in the recognition of the right to professional qualifications, as set out in the law of 4 July 1990. Today, the CFI appears to be a global measure enabling all of those who have no qualifications to acquire some, during a period of unemployment or at work.

General objectives

According to the terms of the law of 4 July 1990, article L 900.3 of the Labour Code specifies that every person in working life has the right to professional qualifications. The person must be able to pursue, on his or her own initiative, a training course which will result in a qualification, whatever the status of the person concerned. The training course must either:

- fall under the law of 16 July 1971 relating to the orientation of technological education (technological diplomas or similar); or
- appear on a list compiled by the joint national employment commission for each professional sector; or
- be recognized in the classifications of a national branch collective agreement.

Implementation of the CFI for jobseekers implies the organization of the following tasks:

- an assessment which makes it possible to map out a training route;
- a personalized training route which is reflected notably in an individual follow-up;
- a system of authentication enabling recognition of the qualifications which have been acquired during the training route.

The training credit is not a new training form. Its implementation depends on the entire range of training initiatives that can be made available, depending on the situation of those interested.

Priorities

Excepting special cases, the CFI applies to those jobseekers aged over 26 years who do not have professional qualifications authenticated by a certificate of vocational aptitude, or by the certificate of vocational studies. The training routes organized in this context aim to steer jobseekers towards a first professional qualification which is recognizable both in France and throughout the rest of the EC. Recipients of the *Minimum Integration Income* (RMI) are eligible for the training credit, whether or not they are registered at the National Employment Agency (ANPE).

With regard to training capacities that can be made available, from 1991 onwards the training credits for unemployed adults are designed to benefit approximately 45,000 jobseekers – 20,000 jobseekers eligible for a Redeployment Training Allowance and 25,000 other jobseekers, with priority given to long-term jobseekers.

Guidance towards the training credit
Adult jobseekers who are interested in the training credit are steered in
the direction of the ANPE, which is responsible for organizing it. The
various options which are available are examined by the ANPE together
with each jobseeker, for whom the absence of qualifications hinders
vocational reintegration with regard to job vacancies. The ANPE
appoints one of its agents as a correspondent for each CFI recipient. This
person is responsible in particular for the elaboration and the individualized follow-up of the training route.

Training route
The elaboration of a personalized training route requires as much a
diagnosis of the experience and training needs of the jobseeker as a
prognosis on the steps necessary to obtain a recognized qualification.

Beyond the activities which the ANPE performs within the framework
of its basic tasks (vocational support, evaluation of the level of vocational
abilities, session of in-depth guidance, etc) the correspondent can
proceed to in-depth assessments of abilities. This assessment is not a
prerequisite to the conclusion of a training credit contract, but a helpful
aid to decision-making.

As soon as the planned training route is finalized between the jobseeker
and the correspondent or agent, the contract is signed by these two
parties and by the head of the training department, on behalf of the state.

Training
Training courses that can be made available for the CFI system,
depending on the situation of the person interested, are:

• run by public institutes and bodies under the supervision of the
  various ministerial departments;
• subsidized or regulated by the state;
• accessible to those receiving the AFR;
• (traineeships or employment contracts) accessible in accordance with
  the programme of training and assistance for the reintegration of
  long-term jobseekers;
• initiatives in the framework of the employment-solidarity contract;
• financed by the territorial authorities, subject to their agreement.

The contents of the personalized training route can be the combination
of several training initiatives of suitable length to ensure progress
towards an authenticated qualification. Excepting special cases, the
length of training prior to receiving a diploma or a vocational title at
(so-called) level V, should be under 1200 hours.

Employment promotion

New measures to promote job creation include the following:

- exemption from contributions for companies with fewer than 500 employees which hire young unqualified persons aged between 18 and 26 years on a permanent contract. Subject to certain conditions, this recruitment gives entitlement to an exemption from employers' contributions for social security, pension funds and unemployment. The exemption is for 100 per cent for the first 12 months and 50 per cent for the following six months;
- permanent exemption from contributions in the case of CRE contracts. Persons receiving the Minimum Integration Wage, aged between 50 and 65 years, who have been unemployed for more than one year, and (in an 18-month period) other RMI beneficiaries who have been unemployed for more than one year (without necessarily having registered at the National Employment Agency, ANPE) can also benefit from this permanent exemption;
- monitoring of jobseekers; a number of measures which formerly appeared in a decree, circular or ANPE regulation are now integrated into the Labour Code. Sanctions in the event of false declarations have been stepped up. Monitoring committees and boards have been set up to chart the progress of trainees, to identify problems, to recommend solutions and to make suggestions for future improvements in the fields of vocational training and integration.

In 1992, the French government decided to boost its economic reintegration efforts in order to assist and promote persons in difficulties, particularly persons who are unemployed or who have been laid off and who are older than 50 years. In order to implement this, the CRE measure has been extended to include:

- persons aged 50 years or over who have been laid off;
- unemployed persons aged 50 years or over, whatever the length of the period of unemployment.

Higher education

The minimum entry qualification to university is the *baccalauréat*, which itself officially constitutes the first higher education diploma. Alternatively, various arrangements are made for university admissions for adults without the *baccalauréat*. Higher education is provided in universities, *grandes écoles* and a number of other institutions (some of which are private). Entry to *grandes écoles* is competitive, and admission relies on proof of previous academic achievements as well as entrance examinations.

University courses in general comprise three study cycles including a series of qualification stages. The first, lasting two years, leads to a general university studies diploma, the *Diplôme d'Études Universitaires Générales* (DEUG), which includes compulsory and optional subjects. The second cycle, also lasting two years (five years for medical subjects), leads to the *licence* after the first and the *maîtrise* (master's degree) after the second year. The third cycle is usually made up of a three-year doctorate or a one-year *Diplôme d'Études Supérieures Spécialisées* (DESS) involving training for a profession.

Universities determine their own courses. State control extends to entrance requirements and minimum content and length of courses. A global sum of money is allocated to a university which it may spend as it thinks fit, subject to government audit and published accounts. In theory, students participate in the running of the universities, and sit on student committees as well as subject department boards.

The *grandes écoles* are specialized higher education institutes; some, such as the *École Polytechnique* and the *École Nationale d'Administration* having more prestige than universities. Many are controlled and financed by government ministries (eg, defence, agriculture), some are postgraduate institutions, and some such as the *Écoles de Haut Enseignement Commercial* (HEC), are private. Most have a scientific or technological specialism. Entrance is highly competitive, normally entailing a two- or three-year course (*cours préparatoires*) run by the *lycées* after the *baccalauréat*, followed by a competitive examination. Courses at the *grandes écoles* usually last from one to three years and lead to diplomas.

Instituts Universitaires de Technologie (IUTs) are specialist and technical institutions which were founded in 1969 and which offer two-year courses leading to a national qualification, the *Diplôme Universitaire de Technologie* (DUT). Each IUT constitutes a faculty of the university to which it is formally linked.

In the *Lycée d'Enseignement Technologique* the qualification of *Brevet de Technicien Supérieur* is available. This is a two-year course of study, very specific in its career orientation, at the same level as the DUT. Entry qualification is the *Baccalauréat du Technicien* or *Brevet de Technicien* gained in the technical system or the *Baccalauréat d' Enseignement Général* taken in the *Lycée d'Enseignement Général*.

Other higher education institutes include *Instituts Nationaux Polytechniques, Instituts Nationaux de Sciences Appliquées, Écoles Nationales Supérieures d'Ingénieurs* as well as various business schools, art schools, music colleges and private educational institutions.

Teacher training

In France, teachers are civil servants, recruited at different levels by competitive examinations before training specifically for the teaching profession. There is a complex hierarchy of teaching staffs in schools which is reflected in the training system. Primary and pre-primary school teachers are trained on three year courses in *Écoles Normales*. Secondary school teachers must hold one of a variety of qualifications, according to the type of subject which they teach. Candidates who wish to proceed to teach must hold a *licence* (national degree awarded on successful completion of the first year of the second university cycle) in the relevant discipline, which may be acquired at a university or at a specialist teacher training institution (IPES). The final examination is in two parts, theory and practice; the latter is taken after professional training lasting one year. A higher qualification, held by some *lycée* or university teachers is the *agrégation*, a very competetive examination, taken after a one-year course for which the entry qualification is the *maîtrise*. There are a number of other categories of teachers for which there are a variety of competitive recruitment examinations and training courses.

Adult education

Adult education is well established in France. All major cities and towns have education services which operate on a flexible learning basis and provide a whole range of vocational and academic courses. People living in rural areas are well served by the sophisticated network of open learning and distance learning educational packages. In addition, the University of the Third Age, U3A is well developed in France and one of its major functions is educational services for older people. Some vocational training and retraining schemes are run by the Ministries of Education and Labour. *'Education permanente'* is a powerful force and a major contributor to vocational training and retraining and some 2 million workers participate annually through the *National Agency for Education Permanente*. There are many voluntary bodies with official support, such as *Peuple et Culture*, which promote courses for adults.

Universities provide both full-time as well as part-time adult education classes. The French government has introduced a number of alternative arrangements with regard to university admissions for adults. The *attestation de réussite à l'examen spécial d'accès aux études universitaires* – ESEU (univeristy entrance exam) is offered to adults, aged 20 or over, without a *baccalauréat* and who have had at least two years' work experience. This examination is offered once a year by the universities and consists of two main components, literature and science. Also, the *validation des acquis* is a specific programme examination which, in certain cases, allows a university to examine the study, work experience and personal knowledge of a given candidate in a specific field. The candidate must be at least 20 years old and submit an application outlining his or her experience and reasons for wanting to pursue a higher education course. If satisfied, the university will allow a candidate to pursue a course.

Employing organizations are obliged by law to devote at least 0.8 per cent of their salary bills to the training of their employees, and many firms have established relationships with local universities in order to train their staff locally. Such training is generally work-related. There is also a higher education scheme for workers which, through evening courses and periods of practical training, allows them to work for a diploma of higher technical studies obtainable after three or four years' study.

ECONOMIC FEATURES

Encompassing some 210,000 square miles of land, France is about four-fifths the size of Texas. It shares borders with six European countries: Spain on the south; Italy, Switzerland and Germany on the east; Luxembourg and Belgium on the north. Across the English Channel is Great Britain, to which France is linked by the Channel Tunnel. With 1700 miles of coastline – along the Atlantic Ocean, Mediterranean Sea and English Channel – France's location provides direct access to Europe's busiest sea lanes. Its ports are worldwide distribution centres. The port of Marseille is the second largest in Europe, after Rotterdam. Le Havre on the English Channel is the fifth largest port in Europe, and its 210 regular lines include over 20 to North America. French transportation infrastructure includes Europe's most extensive rail network, which features the *train à grande vitesse* (TGV), the world's fastest train. In terms of air traffic, Paris is second only to London in passenger traffic and third behind Frankfurt and London for cargo.

Employment promotion measures

The fight against long-term unemployment and exclusion is high on the French government's list of priorities. For this reason it has decided to step up its efforts on behalf of young and adult Long-Term Unemployed (LTUs) and has mobilized the Public Employment Service (SPE) on a major scale, in particular the external services of the Ministry of Labour, the National Employment Agency (ANPE) and the Adult Vocational Training Association (AFPA). The requisite financial and human resources to combat this exclusion phenomenon have also been approved. The plan is therefore that 900,000 LTUs who currently make up over 31 per cent of all unemployed, will be closely monitored by the

ANPE and its partners in the SPE, and that various on-going training schemes and reintegration schemes will be introduced throughout France to attempt to solve the problems of unemployment.

On a local level, the schemes are to be boosted by new resources, and under the terms of agreements made with the General Councils, 250 ANPE officials will be allocated to the RMI support units to assist the RMI instructors who are responsible for the integration contracts which will be drawn up for LTUs who receive the RMI. These officials will receive half of their salary from the state.

A monitoring unit has been set up in each prefecture with representatives from the 'Departmental' Dictorate of Labour, Employment and Vocational Training, the Directorate of Social Affairs, the 'Departmental' Delegation of the ANPE and also the official RMI representative in the prefecture and a representative of the General Council. The monitoring unit meets on a weekly basis and concentrates on the quality of the interviews, of the proposals, of the liaison with the partners and of the follow-up.

The procedure

Every appropriate integration option will be suggested to the jobseeker using all available instruments relating to a job offer, a training offer and general interest offer, in order to direct him or her towards the competent organization or body and thereby promote his or her effective reintegration into employment.

The measures proposed

Three types are proposed:

- training schemes;
- training-cum-work contracts;
- practical assistance schemes.

The training schemes are as follows:

- the Integration and Training Scheme (AIF) which promotes the vocational reintegration of adult LTUs who are experiencing serious integration difficulties; 260,000 places are available and the aim is to bring their vocational skills up to scratch or provide them with new skills. The AFPA has organized 30,000 traineeships under this programme;
- The CREs which provide an incentive to recruit people who have been excluded from the labour market for a long time by granting excemption from employers' contributions and by providing assistance in the form of a lump sum of FF10,000. This scheme has been extended to unemployed persons aged over 50 who have been

looking for employment for at least three months; 150,000 CRE places were available in 1992;

- the programme of active preperation for Qualification and Employment (PAQUE) which is aimed at:
  - young jobseekers under 26 who have been registered at the ANPE for longer than 12 months;
  - young people who have applied to a company or training body and have been turned down as a result of a lack of skills or know-how.
- the Vocational Rehabilitation Traineeships (SRP) which offer jobseekers with work experience the opportunity to extend and bring up to date their vocational skills via a short training programme.
- access to Employment Traineeships which provide jobseekers with the vocational skills to enable them to take up a job offer registered at the ANPE.

With regard to training-cum-work contracts, the various options are as follows:

- matching jobseekers with job offers from the ANPE;
- employment solidarity contracts, which have diversified into new areas such as the environment, transport, the postal service, aid for the sick, leisure promotion activities and safety in urban areas, modernization of communal facilities used by schools and universities;
- guidance contracts which propose training activities in-company or in a training centre;
- qualification and apprenticeship contracts which enable a young person to gain a vocational qualification recognized by a technician diploma or a qualification approved by collective agreement;
- practical assistance in the search for employment comprising sessions on job-search techniques and job-search help groups.

Practical assistance schemes such as Individual Social Support (ASI) enable LTUs who are experiencing difficulties on various fronts (social, health, family, etc) to benefit from individual social support tailored to their particular situation. This watchdog service is provided by the competent bodies. This ambitious plan is testimony to the determination of the government to do everything possible to combat the plague afflicting the European labour market, and particularly the French market, namely long-term unemployment leading to long-lasting social exclusion.

Economic incentives

France is offering cash grants, low-cost loans and tax concessions in the hope that new job creation will reduce the country's high unemployment, currently averaging 9.3 per cent.

Low energy costs

In addition to underwriting some of the costs of new jobs, France is offering incentives to lower overhead costs for business.

France's massive investment in nuclear generating plants has made the country the second-ranking nation, after the USA, in terms of nuclear generating capacity. For industrial users, electricity costs are 30 to 40 per cent lower in France than in other EC nations.

Major financial incentives

Companies that establish locations in France during the country's push to upgrade its regional economies will be eligible for lucrative investment incentives.

The four basic areas of assistance from the French government are: tax concessions, cash grants, low-interest and long-term loans, and accelerated depreciation of capital assets.

Government grants and loans for fixed assets

DATAR, the Paris-based parent agency of the French Industrial Development Agency, provides cash grants, or *Prime d'Amenagement du Territoire* (PAT), that can finance up to 25 per cent of the investment of companies that establish or expand industrial operations. Companies taking over ailing businesses may also benefit from a grant. A PAT grant is available to firms that create at least 20 jobs within the first three years of operation or 10 jobs after a major expansion. The amount of the investment must be at least US$3.6 million and the company's worldwide sales must exceed US$54 million. At the current exchange rate (FF5.55=US$1.00), the PAT grants range from US$6300 to US$9000 per job created.

Government grants are also offered for setting up R&D centres and engineering management and software development operations.

The *Agence Nationale de Valorisation de la Recherche* (ANVAR), a government agency promoting technology innovation and transfer, helps finance research and development projects. Targeted areas include biotechnology, metallurgy, electronics, energy and pollution control. ANVAR provides aid ranging from interest-free advances to subsidies of 50 to 70 per cent of labour and transport costs of consultants and researchers and for training.

Local subsidies

The majority of business parks and industrial zones are owned and operated by municipalities or chambers of commerce, which usually sell or lease the land and may provide financing for existing buildings or construction.

Aid from industrial groups
In addition to investment offered by national, regional and local agencies, a number of France's major corporations have made their own provisions for funding new ventures.

In a concerted effort to attract new business to the areas of France that have been hit hardest by the decline of traditional manufacturing, these firms offer assistance in the form of low-interest, long-term loans as well as job training subsidies and subsidies to new ventures. The industrial groups include, among others, the steel concern USINOR-SACILOR, the oil and gas company Elf-Aquitaine, the construction group Saint Gobain Development, and the French Coal Board, Charbonnages de France. The coal board, for instance, has set up a division, Sofirem, to deliver financial incentives and consulting services to firms investing in France's 11 mining areas.

Training subsidies
Training and retraining can be financed by government funds and, in certain areas, by local sources. Trainees' salaries and benefits, as well as indirect outlays including materials, depreciation of equipment used in training, and salaries and benefits for instructors, are eligible for reimbursement.

Tax exemptions
A corporate tax exemption for the first 10 years of operation is available to companies incorporating and operating in three enterprise zones located at Dunkirk in the north and in the Marseille-Toulon area on the Mediterranean coast. Companies in the zones must employ at least 10 workers after two years of operation. Excluded from this tax benefit are companies involved in a few industrial sectors as well as in banking, insurance, civil engineering contracting and real estate. Corporations taking advantage of enterprise zone status are precluded from government grant programmes.

A partial or total exemption from the business licence tax (*taxe professionnelle*) for up to five years can also be granted, depending on the area selected for the investment.

Job training tax credits and R&D tax credits are also available and there are numerous regions, departments and individual cities that provide investment incentives to foreign firms willing to set up operations in their locales.

Lastly, the European Commission has set up a special programme in

Longwy, on the border of France, Luxembourg and Belgium, that matches DATAR funding with a grant; the combined incentives total up to 37.5 per cent of an investment.

FINDING EMPLOYMENT

EC nationals have the right to live and work in France without a work permit. A full EC passport is required and a visitor's passport or excursion document is not sufficient. If a visitor intends to stay for over three months he or she must apply to the local *Commissariat de Police* or town hall (*la mairie*) for a residence permit (*carte de séjour*). A *carte de séjour* is valid for the period of contracted employment up to 12 months. If an employment contract is issued for longer than 12 months then a *carte de séjour* is issued for five years. The five-year permit is automatically renewable.

EC nationals working in France have the same rights as French nationals with regard to pay, working conditions, access to housing, vocational education and training, trade union membership and social security arrangements. The French employment service, *Agence Nationale pour l'Emploi* (ANPE), has its head office in Paris, and EC nationals can use the service free of charge. ANPE offices are located in all cities and towns throughout France; the address of the nearest can be found in the telephone directory, *Les Pages Jaunes*.

Private employment agencies (*agences de travail temporaire*) cover temporary work only. Major agencies include *Manpower, Bis, Marlar, John Stork* and *Select France*. To register with one of these organizations, a French social security number is required, which can be obtained from the local offices of *Caisse d'Assurance Maladie*.

The French press carries job advertisements. National dailies include *France-Soir, Le Monde* (with its weekly job vacancy supplement called *Initiatives*) and *Le Figaro*, and there are hundreds of regional daily papers as well. In addition, there are several specialist journals and trade magazines. Titles of all of them can be found 'on-line' in major reference libraries. A useful weekly job magazine for junior/middle managers is *Courriers Cadres* produced by the *Association pour l'Emploi des Cadres* (APEC). APEC has offices providing a placement service for professional people including young graduates in over 30 French cities. Useful directories include *Guide des Opportunitiés de Carrières* (often known as 'French Go'), the *Guide des Entreprises qui Recrutent*, and trade directories such as *KOMPASS*. The French telecom system, *Agence Commercials des Télécommunications* (ACT) also has computer terminals which allow direct access to various databases including several holding job vacancies. In France, there is available on Minitel a facility managed by APEC called *Futurum Vitae* which enables job-seekers to input their CVs for employers to access. APEC also produces extensive written information to help jobseekers, including new graduates. The *Association Bernard Gregory* can circulate the CVs of PhD scientists to employers, and runs a vacancy information service which is available on the Minitel system (access 36.14 ABG), all free of charge. It also organizes a biennial recruitment fair called *Eurospore* for PhD scientists. Many institutions also organize their own fairs and will often admit foreign visitors.

Many French employers regard four years of study after the *baccalauréat* as the base line requirement for a graduate-level job; a three-year degree course may not therefore be enough. Fluency in French is required for most jobs. Graphology (handwriting analysis) is a widely used selection technique and French recruiters often require letters to be handwritten. Following pre-selection on paper, graduate applicants in France face similar selection procedures to their counterparts in the rest of the EC (interviews, personality and aptitude tests). These will usually, of course, all be conducted in French.

The French government is closely involved with employment issues. There is a statutory minimum wage, called the *Salaire Minimum Inter-professionel de Croissance* (SMIC). Most employees are paid on a monthly basis, and pay is usually on a 13 or 14 month basis. The normal working week is around 39 hours with overtime legally restricted to a basic maximum of nine hours per week. The minimum holiday entitlement is five weeks. All employees and employers pay contributions to the official sickness, maternity, invalidity and death scheme. They also contribute to a basic pension and at least one additional pension.

INFORMATION POINTS

Education and training

AFREF
Association francaise pour
l'expansion par la formation
56 rue de Londres
75008 Paris

APEC
Association pour l'Emploi des Cadres
51 boulevard Brune
75689 Paris Cedex 14

Association Bernard Gregory
53 rue de Turbigo
75003 Paris

CNAM
Centre de Recherche pour la
Formation
2 rue Conte
75003 Paris

CSN FOR
Chambre Syndicale Nationale des
organismes de formation
20 rue de l'Arcade
75008 Paris

GARF
Groupement des Animateurs et
Responsables de Formation
d'entreprise
12 rue Sainte-Anne,
75001 Paris

INFRO
Tour Europe Cedex 07
92080 Paris-la-Defense

Ministère de l'Education Nationale
Bureau d'Information et
d'Orientation
61/65 rue Dutot
75015 Paris

ORGAFORM
Conseil National des Organismes de
Formation Professionelle
153 blvd Haussmann
75008 Paris

UNORF
Union Nationale des Organismes de
Formation
37 quai de Grenelle
75015 Paris

Employment

ANPE
Le Galilee
4 rue Galilee
93198 Noisy-le-Grand

Caisse Primaire d'Assurance –
Maladie de Paris
Service de Relations Internationales
173-175 rue de Bercy
75586 Paris

European Information Centres

Amiens
Chambre Régionale de Commerce et
D'Industrie de Picardie
Euro Info Centre
36 rue des Otages
80037 Amiens – Cedex

Annecy
(antenne/satellite FR-251)
Chambre de Commerce et
d'Industrie d'Annecy et de la
Haute-Savoie
2 rue du Lac – BP 2072
74011 Annecy

Avignon
(antenne/satellite FR-268)
Chambre de Commerce et
d'Industrie d'Avignon et de Vaucluse
46 cours Jean Jaurès – BP 158
84008 Avignon

Basse-Terre (La Guadeloupe)
Conseil Régional de Guadeloupe
Euro Info Centre
5 rue Victor Hugues
97100 Basse-Terre – La Guadeloupe

Besançon
Chambre Régionale de Commerce et
d'Industrie de Franche-Comté
Euro Info Centre
Valparc
ZAC de Valentin
25043 Besançon

Blagnac
Chambre Régionale de Commerce et
d'Industrie Midi-Pyrénées
Euro Info Centre
5 rue Dieudonné Costes – BP 32
31701 Blagnac

Bordeaux
Comité d'Expansion Aquitaine
Euro Info Centre
2 place de la Bourse
33076 Bordeaux

Caen
Chambre Régionale de Commerce et
d'Industrie de Basse Normandie
Euro Info Centre
26 avenue de Thiès
Pericentre III – BP 5154
14040 Caen

Cayenne (Guyane)
Chambre de Commerce et
d'Industrie de la Guyane
Euro Info Centre
Hôtel Consulaire
place de l'Esplanade – BP 49
97321 Cayenne

Chalons-sur-Marne
CCI de Chalons-sur-Marne
Point Europe 'Champagne Ardenne'
Euro Info Centre
2 rue de Chastillon – BP 533
51010 Chalons-sur-Marne

Clermont-Ferrand
Chambre de Commerce et
d'Industrie de
Clermont-Ferrand/Issoire
Euro Info Centre
148, bd Lavoisier
63037 Clermont-Ferrand

Dijon
Chambre Régionale de Commerce et
d'Industrie de Bourgogne
Euro Info Centre
68 rue Chevreul – BP 209
21006 Dijon

Fort-de-France (La Martinique)
Chambre de Commerce et
d'Industrie de La Martinique
Euro Info Centre
50 rue Ernest Deproge – BP 478
97241 Fort-De-France
La Martinique

Grenoble
(antenne/satellite FR-251)
Chambre de Commerce et
d'Industrie de Grenoble
GREX
1 place A. Malraux – BP 297
38016 Grenoble

Lille
Conseil Régional ARD / Maison des
Professions/CCI
Euroguichet Nord Pas de Calais
Centre de Documentation
185 boulevard de la Liberté – BP
2027
59013 Lille

Limoges
Chambre Régionale de Commerce et
d'Industrie
Limousin/Poitou/Charentes
Euro Info Centre
boulevard des Arcades
87038 Limoges

Lyon
Chambre de Commerce et
d'Industrie de Lyon
Euro Info Centre
16 rue de la République
69289 Lyon

Marseille
Somecin
Euro Info Centre
2 rue Henri-Barbusse
Mezzanine
13241 Marseille

Metz
Région de Lorraine
Euro Info Centre
place Gabriel Hocquard
BP – 1004
57036 Metz

Montpellier
Comité Liaison Chambres Econom
Languedoc Rousillion – Région
Euro Info Centre
254 rue Michel Teule
ZAC d' Alco – BP 6076
34030 Montpellier

Nantes
Chambre de Commerce et
d'Industrie de Nantes
Euroguichet Entreprises
Centre des Salorges
16, quai Ernest Renaud – BP 718
44027 Nantes

Nice
(antenne/satellite FR-268)
Chambre de Commerce et d'Industrie
Nice Côte d'Azur
20, boulevard Carabacel – BP 259
06005 Nice

Orléans
Chambre Régionale de Commerce et
d'Industrie du Centre/ CRCE
Euro Info Centre
35 avenue de Paris
45000 Orléans

Paris
Agence Nationale de Valorisation de
la Recherche (ANVAR)
Euro Info Centre
43 rue de Caumartin
75436 Paris

Centre Français du Commerce
Extérieur
Euro Info Centre
10 avenue d'Léna
75783 Paris 16

Chambre de Commerce et
d'Industrie de Paris
Chambre Régionale de Commerce et
d'Industrie d'Ile-de-France
Euro Info Centre – Point Europe
2 rue de Viarmes
75001 Paris

Ministère de l'Industrie et de
l'Aménagement du Territoire
Euro Info Centre
84 rue de Grenelle
75353 Paris

Pointe-à-Pitre (La Guadeloupe)
Chambre de Commerce et
d'Industrie de Pointe-à-pitre
BP 64
97152 Pointe-à-Pitre Cedex
La Guadeloupe

Poitiers
Association Poitou-Charentes-Europe
Euro info Centre
47 rue du Marché – BP 229
86006 Poitiers

Rennes
Chambre Régionale de Commerce et
d'Industrie de Bretagne
Euro Info Centre
1 rue du Général Guillaudot
35044 Rennes

Rouen
Chambre Régionale de Commerce et
d'Industrie de Haute Normandie
Euro Info Centre
9 rue Robert Schuman – BP 124
76002 Rouen

Saint Denis (La Reunion)
Chambre de Commerce et
d'Industrie de La Réunion
Euro Info Centre
5 bis, rue de Paris – BP 120
97463 Saint Denis

Strasbourg
Chambre de Commerce et
d'Industrie de Strasbourg et du
Bas-Rhin
Euro Info Centre
10 place Gutenberg – BP 444 R8
67008 Strasbourg

Chapter 5

Germany

KEY FACTS

Surface area	357,041 sq km, 137,853 sq miles
Capital	Berlin
Major towns	Cologne, Munich, Essen, Frankfurt-am-Main, Dortmund, Stuttgart, Dusseldorf, Leipzig, Dresden, Chemnitz, Magdeburg; Ports Hamburg, Kiel, Cuxhaven, Bremerhaven, Rostock
Form of government	democratic federal republic
Population	(1990 est) 77,600,000, annual growth rate 0.7 per cent
Language	German
Currency	Deutschmark
Exports	machine tools (world's leading exporter), cars, commercial vehicles, electronics, industrial goods, textiles, chemicals, iron, steel, wine, lignite, uranium, cobalt, coal, fertilizers, plastics
Vocational educational institutions	training company and part-time vocational schools (*Berufsschulen*)

Awarding organizations	Chamber of Industry and Commerce (IHK), Chamber of Handicrafts (HWK), Guild or Vocational School
Grants	means-tested maintenance support in the form of grants; some scholarships
Vocational qualifications	certificate awarded by a Chamber of Industry and Commerce, a Chamber of Handicrafts, a Guild or a Vocational School
Trends/developments	increased financial incentives towards continuing vocational training have been introduced under the Vocational Training Act. Inspection teams have been appointed to ensure the quality and efficiency of vocational training and qualifications. In 1991, a study undertaken by CEDEFOP revealed a trend amongst young people in Germany to opt for a more classical education rather than to enter the dual system, which is often considered by other countries to be the model of good practice

EDUCATION SYSTEM

The main responsibility for educational policy and development of services lies with individual state (*länder*) governments. Most young children attend some kind of voluntary pre-primary schooling. There are three types of pre-primary schooling; the main one, the kindergarten, caters for children aged 3 to 5, while in some *länder* primary schools have preparatory and reception classes (*vorklassen*) for 5-year-olds. School-based kindergartens also cater for children of compulsory school age who may be not quite mature enough for primary education.

Although responsibility for kindergartens lies mainly within the remit of the Ministry of Health, Family, Youth and Social Affairs, four-fifths of the funding is from private sources, including the church. Nominal fees are payable, but in practice only by those who can afford them. Staff are either teachers, social education workers or children's nurses.

Compulsory education

Compulsory full-time education lasts from ages 6 to 15 in three main phases: four years primary, then two years' secondary education before final selection into one of four further types of upper secondary schools. Those pupils leaving at 15 must continue in compulsory part-time education for a further three years, mainly in *berufsschulen* (vocational schools)

The school year is divided by 12 weeks' holiday: two each in autumn, Christmas and Easter and six in the summer. Most schools work a six-day week, in the morning alone, plus occasional extra-curricular afternoon activities, but there is an increasing number of full-day schools on a five-day week. The 'morning' system runs from 8.00 to 14.00 including a short snack break. Pupils are set homework which parents are intended to supervise, and home advice and assistance is expected to reinforce schooling. Pupils whose parents are both working can attend child-minding establishments (*kinderhörte*) providing play facilities and home-work supervision and help.

Primary education

Primary school begins at age 6 and continues for four years, and concentrates on the 3Rs, supplemented by compulsory lessons in religious knowledge, local studies, music, art, craft and physical education. In the first two years there are 20–26 periods weekly, extending to 24–30 in the last two. The primary school recommends, in consultation with the parents, the most suitable type of secondary school for each pupil. However, this is only a recommendation and parents are free to challenge the advice given. The child than attends a school of their parents' choice, but must pass a test after a probationary period in order to be accepted as a permanent pupil. Ample provision is made for pupil transfer between the different types of school.

Secondary education

Secondary education consists of two phases, beginning with a two-year 'orientation' phase, with a common curriculum, intended to aid transfer between types of school, as appropriate. The four main types of lower secondary school are as follows.

1. *Hauptschulen* (secondary modern): over 40 per cent of primary school children transfer to a *hauptschulen* which provides education up to the age of 15. The *hauptschulen* aims to introduce less-academic children to the working world, with a wide curriculum including science and one foreign language. About 80 per cent of

such pupils gain a school leaving certificate, qualifying them for either apprenticeships or continuing their full-time education.

2. *Realschulen* (technical grammar): offer classes to age 16 which can lead by examination (Intermediate Certificate) to upper secondary school or to employment. About 28 per cent of primary pupils go to these increasingly popular schools. The curriculum is more demanding than in the *hauptschulen* and is also more varied; another foreign language, a second science subject and often business studies are included alongside the standard curricular subjects. Such schools offer a safe route to middle management jobs, or continuing full time education.

3. *Gymnasien* (grammar): offer academic courses to age 19 leading to higher education. About 31 per cent of pupils transfer into the lower stage of higher education. Such schools are specialized and the original three categories – classical, modern languages and scientific – have been joined by various vocational courses, such as engineering, music, domestic science, etc. Some *gymnasien* cater specifically for those pupils transferring from the two types of school previously described. Pupils are usually streamed, and it is common for many pupils to repeat a year, since advancement to the next class depends on a strict marking system for tests and classwork. Pupils leaving at 15 are awarded, on satisfactory performance, an intermediate certificate, similar to that gained in the *realschule*; the main *gymnasien* examination is the *abitur*.

4. *Gesamtschulen* (comprehensive): two main types predominate – the integrated school and the cooperative type. The latter incorporates the three basic types of school described above on one site, sometimes under one head teacher, but with coordinated curricula to facilitate transfers between school types. In the integrated comprehensive, pupils are taught together, but streamed for the basic subjects.

Special schools

All children are entitled to education and training, and arrangements for pupils with physical or learning disabilities range from special classes in general schools, to various modes in special schools, half-day, all-day or boarding. The precise system varies between each *land* and between forms of disability. Except for provision for children and young people with severe learning disabilities, special schools/classes use the standard curriculum, with teaching methodology specially adapted to various handicaps.

Administration

The German government has developed broad principles and priorities in education and has its main legislative responsibility in the post-compulsory area, to oversee the inservice part of vocational training, and support certain aspects of higher education, such as capital costs and scientific research. Each *land* has its own Ministry of Education and Cultural Affairs which interprets the national framework in its own constitution. Each *land* draws up its own syllabus, recommends textbooks, and organizes its schools and teaching, without any system of national inspection. All examinations, including the *abitur*, are local and the *länder* authorities also train, appoint and promote teachers.

Finance

Public expenditure on education accounts for some 5 per cent of GNP. In addition, the Health Ministry supports pre-schooling, and is aided by the private sector. Educational expenditure is mainly met by the *länder* (70 per cent), 23 per cent by local district authorities and 7 per cent by the government.

Compulsory state education is free; no *länder* charge fees and most provide free teaching material such as textbooks, stationery and free school transport where necessary. Means-tested grants and scholarships are available for older pupils, including those in vocational training and higher education. Only around 4 per cent of pupils attend private schools (often boarding) which must be state approved, and may, in some *länder*, receive a little financial support.

Schools are funded locally at district level, except for teachers' salaries which are met by the *länder*. The federal government contributes little towards school-level education. The school-based element of vocational training is funded by the *länder*, but the inservice or employer-based part is funded by the industry concerned.

At university level, the federal government contributes about a third of the running costs, and around one half of the capital costs of a new college.

VOCATIONAL EDUCATION SYSTEM

Post-compulsory education

Some nine out of ten 16-year-old school leavers in Germany receive vocational training and almost three quarters of 16- to 18-year-olds do so as apprentices, through the so called 'Dual System' combining on-the-job and off-the-job training. All pupils not continuing in general education must attend one of various secondary schools (*berufsschule*) for compulsory vocational education at least on a part-time basis and for at least three years. The first of these three years may be full-time or the whole three years may be spent under the dual-system (up to 12 hours per week school instruction plus on-the-job training). About a quarter of all apprentices go on to train as *meister* – fully trained workers with at least two years' work experience and then a further one or two years' training.

Regional states or *länder* are responsible for vocational training in schools but the government is responsible for the various forms of vocational training outside schools, that is, on-the-job training under the Vocational Training Act 1969 and the Craft Regulations 1965. Introduced in 1991, the Vocational Education and Training Promotion Act has become the new legal basis for the annual Vocational Education and Training Report. The *Bundess-Institut für Berufsbildung* (BIBB – Federal Institute for Vocational Education and Training) was revised in 1992 in line with the new legislation. The aim of the new amendments is to make the work of the BIBB more efficient and to adapt to new vocational requirements, in particular to enable more international co-operation in the field of vocational education and training. The new federal *länder* will be involved in the work of the governing body, 'the Board', which comprises representatives of employers' and employees' organizations, the federal government and the *länder*. Some of the Board's tasks have been transferred to a newly established 'Standing Committee'. The new Vocational Training Act places increased emphasis in future on questions relating to quality, structure, finance, employment and regulation policy of all aspects of vocational education and training.

German legislation relating to vocational education and training applies to vocational training courses in industry and agriculture and comparable non-industrial institutions, for example, the civil service, and some professions. These individual enterprises may themselves provide training programmes (governed by law) but there are vocational training centres run by a multiplicity of organizations, eg, employers' organizations, Chambers of Trade or Commerce, and (in Cologne) the *Handwerkskammer* (Chamber of Handicrafts), which is the largest in Germany. These latter training centres tend to provide those aspects of training which individual enterprises cannot provide.

Vocational training contracts are made between the firm (known as the instructor) and the trainee. The subject matter, length of vocational training (usually three years), and assessment requirements are governed by law. On completion of training for a recognized occupation, the trainee takes a final examination administered by the Chamber for Arts and Crafts for the trades sector, Chambers of Industry and Commerce for industrial and commercial occupations and the Chambers of Agriculture for farming occupations. The chambers are self-regulatory public corporations, membership of which is compulsory for all commercial enterprises. The chambers examine, and often provide courses themselves on behalf of the government in their particular field. The assessment involves a practical exercise, oral and written examinations; candidates must perform satisfactorily in all three elements to qualify. It is perhaps the central place of the chambers in vocational education and training which marks out Germany from the other systems in operation in the EC. What is also noteworthy about the German system is the high level of cooperation and involvement of employers and employees (through their representative bodies) in the whole system of vocational education and training. In fact, there is evidence that employers are maintaining even closer contact with the vocational schools and curricula because of their overall responsibility for ensuring that each apprentice is properly trained. Consequently, there is a huge input of resources into vocational education and training.

The Dual System

Pupils who leave school at the end of compulsory full-time education are obliged to continue their vocational education up to age 18 for one or two days a week at a *berufsschule* (see below). Employers provide the practical training, sometimes in group training centres, and the *länder* governments are responsible for theoretical training through the *berufsschule*. Trainees must receive instruction in one of about 460 legally recognized occupations and must take an examination at the end of training. Success in this examination is a prerequisite for employment at the national standard wage. Success can also provide the gateway to higher level training.

Types of upper secondary school

1. *Berufsschulen* (part-time vocational schools) cater for most young school-leavers, mainly those undergoing vocational training in industry or employed without on-the-job training. Also, a basic vocational training year provides full-time training in a chosen occupational area and satisfactory completion counts towards a normal apprenticeship.

   Vocational schools are attended on a part-time basis, on one or more days a week, for 12 lessons at most, or else full-time for several weeks, on a block release basis. About 40 per cent of the time is devoted to the continuation of general education, in German, social studies, economics, religious studies and sport. The remaining time is devoted to vocational studies specific to the trade. Successful completion of the course gives access to *fachschulen*.

2. *Berufsfachschulen* (full-time vocational schools) receive students from *hauptschulen* and *realschulen* for one or two years. Schools specializing in different vocations exist and all courses end with an examination, which can lead either to higher vocational training or a shortened apprenticeship.

3. *Berufsaufbauschulen* (continuation part-time vocational schools). These schools cater for young people undergoing vocational training or who have completed it. The teaching is at a higher level than the *berufsschule*, leading to the equivalent of the *realschule* intermediate certificate.

4. *Fachoberschulen* (technical high schools) provide a full-time two-year course for *realschule* pupils, leading to higher education.

5. *Berufliche gymnasien* (vocational grammar schools) are for *realschule* pupils. They provide courses with a vocational bias for entry to higher education.

6. *Fachschulen* are schools for those pupils with initial vocational qualifications and offer advanced vocational training as well as general education. They prepare students to manage enterprises in their chosen fields (the trades, agriculture, hotel and catering, domestic sciences).

7. *Gymnasien* extend across both the upper and lower secondary phases, preparing pupils for higher education, and are attended in the upper phase by about 20 per cent of all pupils. Special programmes are available for the more able *hauptschulen* and *realschulen* pupils, and some *gesamtschulen* may also continue to 19.

The final examination undertaken by most pupils at the *gymnasien* is the *abitur*, and provides entry to higher education. Originally the *abitur* consisted of a demanding test in all subjects; there were written examinations in at least four subjects, German, mathematics, one foreign language, plus another foreign language or physics or chemistry; other subjects were examined orally. Under the new system, pupils choose from various broad subject fields, and the final *abitur* consists of written examinations in two main subjects, and one optional subject, plus oral examination in another option. The range must include a modern foreign language, mathematics or natural science and German. The grading system takes account of course work as well as the final examination and main courses are weighted in the ratio of 3:1 to basic courses.

Higher education

Some 1.5 million students annually participate in higher education, which can take place in various types of institutions, taking at least four to five years in any type of university and three to four years elsewhere. There are several higher education establishments without university status, nine theological colleges, 17 colleges of education and 26 fine arts and music institutions.

Fachhochsculen (higher technical colleges), set up in 1968, offer a wide range of three- or four-year courses, directed to practical applications, especially in engineering or commerce. They represent a major part of the German higher education system. *Fachhochschulen* have the task of preparing students for professional activities on the basis of application-related teaching.

The prerequisite for access to studies at universities and equivalent institutions of higher education is proof of having a university entrance qualification, generally acquired after 13 years of schooling. Entry to higher education is normally by gaining an *abitur*, via the *gymnasien*, but other options are also available. An *abitur* can be gained by night school or by schools attached to a university, intended mainly for foreign students. Entrance can also be gained by progressing through the vocational schools described above. In theory, possession of an *abitur* guarantees entry to higher education, but in practice, due to pressure on places, entry to some more popular faculties (medicine and related subjects) depends on merit and also on seniority, to those waiting longest for entry. Foreign EC nationals have free access to all subjects on the basis of their secondary school leaving certificate. In subjects with admission restrictions, a special quota of from 6 per cent to 8 per cent of total available enrolment capacity is reserved for foreign students.

Teacher training

Teacher training is geared either to a specific type of school, or to a particular stage of education. The course takes at least three years (four years for the second level of the second stage and special schools) plus one to one and a half years practical work experience, each phase ending with an examination. Practising teachers are required to attend inservice training in order to extend their qualifications and keep them up to date. Courses are usually residential, for which teachers are granted paid leave.

Staff involved in practical work at vocational training schools qualify first in this aspect at both basic and advanced levels and then undertake theoretical teacher training.

Qualifications

Students present themselves for examination when they feel ready for it, but one check on course length is the grant system which is tied to a fixed study period. There are two basic phases: two or three years of foundation studies leading to the preliminary examination (eg, *Vordiplom*) plus at least two or three further years to the *diplom* or *magister artium*. A doctorate can be gained after two to four years' further study, by a dissertation and oral examination. Those wishing to take up university teaching must also produce a thesis.

The *fachhochschule* course includes practical training and leads to the title *graduiert*, lower than a *diplom*, but granting exemption from at least one year of a *diplom* course to those wishing to transfer. Normally such students proceed directly into employment.

Adult education

Traditionally adult education centres have provided evening classes to adults wishing to extend their education as a leisure activity. However, such centres increasingly augment school leaving qualifications or retrain adults for new jobs. Employers and training organizations are encouraged by the government to cooperate and work together towards combating long term unemployment through providing multiskills training and retraining courses for adults.

Locally based adult education courses enable students to qualify for higher education, with a three- to four-year full- or part-time course. Applicants must be 19 years old, have completed a course of vocational training or have at least three years' regular employment experience. Many towns have modern, purpose-built adult education centres, but extensive use is made of other buildings, mainly schools and higher education institutions.

Internationalization of vocational education

Education and employing organizations in Germany have jointly developed a number of vocational programmes aimed at specialist and managerial personnel from Germany, other industrial nations, and developing countries everywhere. *Carl Duisberg Gesellschaft* (CDG) is one such organization, funded jointly by industry and goverment. It is a non-profit organization for international advanced professional and vocational training and human resource development. CDG undertakes tailor-made programmes for industry and commerce provided that they are work-related, for example, by finding suitable work placements in German firms for other students and exchange employees from other EC countries or long-term work placements in other countries for German students or apprentices. Training programmes usually run for three or four months.

In general, the level at which CDG operates is *fachhochschule*/university level. CDG also operates the German–British Apprenticeship Exchange Programme. Eligible exchange partners are:

- *German side*: Training firms, group training centres, chambers of industry, commerce and skilled crafts, craft training centres.

- *British side*: sponsors of technical and vocational training programmes, in particular colleges of further education and technical colleges.

High demand for vocational counselling in East and West

During the counselling period 1990/91, 1.57 million young people turned to the counselling services of the employment offices with questions about their future working lives; 280,000 of these young people came from the new federal states.

The decision to request a counselling interview apparently has little to do with the situation on the apprenticeship and labour markets. Counselling experts are in demand whether one has difficulties in choosing from the many training opportunities which are available, or if one wants to find the best solution when possibilities are limited. The high number of young people who make use of vocational counselling in the new federal states points towards the growing competence and acceptance of the counselling offered in employment offices.

ECONOMIC FEATURES

In 1991, two reports published by the *Institut der Deutschen Wirtschaft* (the research organization attached to the German employers' associations) cast some interesting light on German economic performance. They revealed that Germany has the highest average real labour costs among comparable countries – DM 37.88 in salary and overheads, compared to DM 24.72 in Britain and similar levels in Japan, France and the US. They also showed that German workers work fewer hours than workers in other countries. They have a poor record of absences due to sickness and similar causes – 9 per cent of annual working time, compared to 7 per cent in the UK, 3 per cent in the US and 1.6 per cent in Japan. Among the countries studied the proportions were higher only in Ireland, Norway and Sweden.

But in spite of high labour costs and relatively high rates of absenteeism, the enlarged German economic market represents a buoyant part of the European Community's infrastructure. The Germany of the future will be economically even stronger than it is today, and in population will represent nearly a quarter of the European Community. To have an establised customer base in such an influential economy would represent a sound business strategy for many other Member State companies.

Employment measures

In January 1992, a number of amendments to the Labour Promotion Act

(AFG) came into force. The introduction of a new Partial Maintenance
Allowance will ensure a better combination of direct job-creation measures with those of continuous vocational training. The financial benefits
granted by the Employment Service make it possible for participants of
a so-called part-time ABM (*Teilzeit-Arbeitbeschaffungsmabnahme*) to
undertake a part-time vocational training measure at the same time. The
combination of training-cum-work provides the employees, on the one
hand, with additional qualifications to enhance their placement chances
and on the other, the opportunity to consolidate and reinforce what is
learned by applying it in practice. The best place to implement the
training-cum-work model is under the framework of the Labour
Promotion, Employment and Structural Development Enterprises
(*Gesellschaften fur Arbeitsforderung, Beschaftigung und Strukturen-
twicklung* – ABS) in the new federal states. They can be realized in these
enterprises with only marginal administrative efforts to support the restructuring process.

Unemployment assistance

Self-service in employment offices
In 1991, the initial phases of the nationwide installation of the Job Information Service (SIS) commenced. The SIS is a self-service system whereby
jobseekers can sift through vacancies themselves. The job offers they
choose from are updated daily. In the SIS, each job offer is registered with
the full name, address and telephone number of the company concerned.
The users can retrieve the job offers on a screen and telephones are
available so that jobseekers can contact employers immediately.

SIS underwent thorough testing in a two-year pilot scheme which was
held in five differently structured employment offices. The acceptance by
employees and employers surpassed all expectations. As a result of the
SIS, labour market partners now make more use of the employment
offices. At the same time, vacancies are filled faster and individual
periods of unemployment have been shortened.

The Federal Employment Service (BA) considers the SIS to be an addition to the traditional placement procedure and not a substitute for it.
Those who wish to continue to make use of a placement officer may of
course do so. However, with the new service, jobseekers can themselves
determine to what extent they want to make use of the job placement
and job counselling department of the employment office.

FINDING EMPLOYMENT

EC nationals have the right to live and work in Germany without a work permit. Full EC passports are essential; a visitor's passport or excursion document is not sufficient. EC nationals are free to enter Germany for up to three months to look for work or set up in business. Visitors, even if looking for work, may be asked to prove that they have adequate financial means for the duration of their stay and that the cost of their return journey is secured. EC nationals taking up residence in Germany must register with their local Registration Office (*Einwohnermeldeamt*) within the first week of arrival. Residence permits are required if a visitor intends to stay for more than three months. Preliminary applications for a residence permit must be made at the *Einwohnermeldeamt.* Only after a preliminary application is endorsed by the local authority is it possible to apply for a residence permit from the Foreign Nationals Authority (*Ausländerbehorde*), which is located in the *Rathaus* (town hall), or the *Kreisverwaltung* (Area Administrative centre). If the application is successful a five-year residence permit (*Aufenthaltsgenehmigung*) is granted.

EC nationals working in Germany have the same rights as nationals of that country with regard to pay, working conditions, access to housing, vocational education and training, social security and trade union membership. In the past, many non-German citizens have taken up work in teaching posts or jobs such as au pairing or hotel work, and a significant number have also entered the German manufacturing industries. To work in the hotel or catering industry, a health certificate is a legal requirement. This can be obtained from the local health department (*Gesundheitsamt*), and there is a charge for the medical examination.

In Germany, the job centre is called the *Arbeitsamt* (AB) and EC nationals can use it free of charge. *Arbeitsamt* offices can be found in all major towns and cities and many smaller towns have sub-offices which are staffed on a part-time basis; addresses are in the telephone directory, *Gelbe Seiten*. The state monopoly of placement activities is organized by the *Bundesanstalt für Arbeit* (BFA) and has offices all over Germany. The central placement office, *Die Zentralstelle für Arbeitsvermittlung* (ZAV) can advise foreign jobseekers as to the likelihood of their getting employment in Germany. They publicize graduates' details to employers in a free weekly newspaper *Markt und Chance* which is in two versions: one with details about jobseekers and one with details about jobs. The European Patent Office based in Munich advertises regularly for engineers and scientists.

There are very few private recruitment firms (*Stellenvermittlingsbüro*) in Germany. However, in the major cities a few agencies have been set up including *Adia, Manpower* and *Interim*.

German daily newspapers are produced on a regional basis, and many carry job advertisements. Examples are *Hamburger Abendblatt, Berliner*

Morgenpost, BZ, Frankfurter Allgemeine Zeitung (Wednesdays), *Bild, Die Welt* and *Handelsblatt*. Weekly newspapers such as *Die Zeit* (Thursdays, for academic posts) and *Welt am Sonnag* also contain jobs pages. Directories of German firms recruiting graduates include *Absolventon Jahrbuch* available in three editions (*Electroteknik/ Informatik, Maschinenwesen/Chimie* and *Wirtschaft/Informatik*) and *Berufsplanung für den Management*. Beyond these, trade directories may be a useful source of information, particularly for engineering and technological jobs.

Recruitment fairs are another way of making contact with employers for graduates resident in Germany. There are generally between 15 and 20 such fairs each year, spread quite evenly throughout the *länder*. When approaching an employer, the CV (in German) should not include hobbies or extra-curricular activities, but should be accompanied by a photograph, a handwritten letter, copies of relevant certificates and a testimonial. This material is generally returned to unsuccessful applicants so that it can be used again. Fluency in German is usually necessary, although this is less crucial in some highly technical jobs or those with international firms.

In Germany, most salary structures are determined by collective bargaining and usually have the force of law. The normal working week is 36–40 hours with overtime rates set by collective agreements. Statutory leave is 25–30 days and agreed between the employee and the employer.

INFORMATION POINTS

Education and training

Bundesverband der Lehrer an beruflichen Schulen (Federal Association of Vocational School Teachers)
An der Esche 2
5300 Bonn 1

Bundesverband der Lehrer an Wirtschaftsschulen
(Federal Association of Commercial School Teachers)
Flemmingstr 11
1000 Berlin 41

Bundesverband Deutscher Berufsbilder
(Federal Association of German Vocational Trainers)
Ludwig-Thoma-Str. 5–7
8510 Furth 2

Carl Duisberg Gessellschaft (CDG)
Holenstraufeuring 30-32
5000 Koln 1

Employment

Chamber of
Commerce/Industrie-und
Handelskammer
British Chamber of Commerce
Heumarkt 14
5000 Koln 1

Zentralstelle für Arbeitsvermittlung
(ZAV) (German employment service)
Fuerubachstrasse 42-46
6000 Frankfurt am Main 1

European Information Centres

Aachen
Industrie und Handelskammer zu
Aachen
Euro Info Centre
Theaterstrasse 6-8
Postf. 650
5100 Aachen

Berlin
Berliner Absatz-Organisation GmbH
Euro Info Centre
Hardenbergstrasse 16-18
1000 Berlin 12

Deutschland Informationszentrum für
Technische Regein (DITR) im DIN e.v
Euro Info Centre
Burggrafenstrasse 6 – Post. 1107
1000 Berlin 30

Bielefeld
Stadt Bielefeld
Euro Info Centre
Niederwall 23
Postf. 181
4800 Bielefeld 1

Bonn
DIHT (Deutscher Industrie-und
Handelstag)
EG-Berantungstelle für Unternehmen
Adenauerallee 148
Postf. 1446
5300 Bonn 1

Deutscher Handwerkskammertag
(DHKT)
EG-Beratungsstelle für Unternehmer
Haus des Deutschen Handwerks
Johanniterstrasse 1
5300 Bonn 1

EG-Beratungsstelle für Unternehmen
Beim
Deutschen Sparkassen-und
Giroverband
Adenauerallee 110
5300 Bonn 1

Genossenschaftliche EG
Beratungs-und
Informationsgesellschaft GEBI mbH
Rheinweg 67
5300 Bonn 1

(antenne/satellite DE-15)
Omnibera
WirtschaftsBeratungsgesellschaft
Coburger Strabe 1C
5300 Bonn

Bremen
VDI/VDE Technologiezentrum
Informations-Technik GmbH
Geschäftsstelle Bremen
EG-Beratungsstelle für Unternehmen
Hanseatenhof 8
2800 Bremen 1

Dresden
Deutsche Gesellschaft für
Mittelstandsberatung GmbH
Euro Info Centre
Zwinglistrabe 36
8020 Dresden

Dusseldorf
Gesellscaft für Wirtscaftsförderung
Nordrhein-Westfalen mbH
Euro Info Centre
Kavalleriestrasse 8–10
Postf. 200309
4000 Dusseldorf

Erfurt
Ostdeutsce Sparkassen-und
Giroverband
Deutsche Girozentrale-Deutsche
Kommunalbank
Euro Info Centre
Am Anger 12
Postf. 167
5010 Erfurt

Frankfurt/Oder
EG-Beratungsstelle für
Unternehmen, bei der Industrie und
Handelskammer Frankfurt/Oder
Euro Info Centre
Humboldstrasse 3 – Postf. 343
1200 Frankfurt/Oder

Hamburg
RKW (Rationalisierungs-Kuratorium
der Deutschen Wirtschaft)
EG-Beratungsstelle für Unternehmen
Heilwigstrasse 33
2000 Hamburg 20

Hannover
Technologie-Centrum Hannover
GmbH
Euro Info Centre
Vahrenwalderstrasse 7
3000 Hannover 1

Kiel
Investitionsbank Schleswig-Holstein
RKW Schleswig-Holstein
EG-Beratungsstelle, EIC
Fleethörn 29–31
Postf. 1128
2300 Kiel 1

Koln
Bundesstelle für
Aubenhandels-Information (BFAI)
Euro Info Centre
Agrippastrasse 87–93
Postf. 108007
5000 Koln 1

EBZ – Europäisches
Beratungs-Zentrum der Deutschen
Wirtschaft
Gustav Heinemann Ufer 84–88
5000 Koln 51

Lahr
Industrie-und Handelskammer
Südlicher Oberrhein
Euro Info Centre
Lotzbechstrasse 31
7630 Lahr

Leipzig
Industrie-und Handelskammer zu
Leipzig (IHK)
Euro Info Centre – EG
Beratungsstelle für Unternehmen
Friedrich-Engels-Platz 5
Postf. 7000
7010 Leipzig

Magdeburg
Handwerkskammer Magdeburg
Euro Info Centre
Humboldstrasse 16
Posf. 1720
3014 Magdeburg

Mulheim
Zenit (Zentrum in
Nordhein-Westfalen für Innovation
und Technik GMBH)
EG-Beratungsstelle für Unternehmen
Dohne, 54
4330 Mulheim Ruhr 1

Munchen
Deutsche Gesellschaft für
Mittelstandsberatung mbH
Euro Info Centre
Arabellastrasse 11
8000 Munchen

Nurnberg
Landesgewerbeanstalt Bayern
OTTI/WETTI/LGA
Euro Info Centre
Karolinenstrasse 45
8500 Nurnberg 1

Ösnabruck
(antenne/satellite DE-110)
Landkreis Ösnabrück Amt fur
Wirtschaftsforderung und
Fremdenverkehr
Am Schölerberg 1
4500 Ösnabruck

Potsdam
Wirtschaftsforderung Bradenburg
GmbH
Euro Info Centre / EG-Beratungsstelle
Am Lehnitzsee
1501 Neufahrland-Polux

Regensburg
Industrie-und Handelskammer
Regensburg
EG-Beratungsstelle für Unternehmen
D. Martin Luther Strasse 12
Postf. 110 355
8400 Regensburg

Rostock
Industrie-und Handelskammer
Rostock
EG-Beratungsstelle
Ernst Barlachstrasse 7
2500 Rostock

Saarbrücken
Zentrale für Produktivitat und
Technologie Saar
Euro Info Centre
Frans Josef Röder Strasse 9
6600 Saarbrücken 1

Steinfurt
(antenne/satellite NL-455)
Kreis Steinfurt
Amt für Wirtschaft und Verkehr
Tecklenburger Strasse 10
4430 Steinfurt

Stuttgart
RKW Rationisierungskuratorium
der Deutschen
Wirtschaft/Landesgruppe Baden
Württemberg
Euro Info Centre
Königstrasse 49
7000 Stuttgart 1

Trier
Technologie-Zentrum Trier
EG-Beratungsstelle für
Rheinland-Pfalz
Gottbillstrasse 34A
5500 Trier

Wiesbaden
Hessische Landesentwicklungs-und
Treuhandgesellscaft mbH
Euro Info Centre
Abraham Lincoln Strasse 38–42
Posf. 3107
6200 Wiesbaden

Chapter 6

Greece

KEY FACTS

Surface area	131,957 sq km, 50,949 sq miles
Capital	Athens
Major towns	ports Thessaloniki, Patras, Larisa, Iráklion
Form of government	democratic republic
Population	(1990 est)10,066,000, annual growth rate 0.3 per cent
Language	Greek
Currency	Drachma
Exports	tobacco, fruit, vegetables, olives, olive oil, textiles
Vocational educational institutions	OAED Accelerated Vocational Training Schools and Centres; Technical and Vocational Lycea; Single and Multi-faculty Lycea
Awarding organization	OAED; Ministry of National Education and Religion
Grants	grants and scholarships available; under the quota system which operates in higher education these may also be available for foreign students

Vocational qualifications	OAED Accelerated Training Certificate; Technical and Vocational Lyceum Diploma; Single or Multi-faculty Diploma
Trends/developments	the general philosophy in vocational education is towards decentralization, greater flexibility and more occupation-specific training curricula

EDUCATION SYSTEM

The education and training systems of Greece are undergoing a dramatic transformation and restructuring; the following account provides an overview of current developments and initiatives in the field of vocational education and training. The system is basically centralized, governed by national laws and by decrees which cover the organization of educational institutions, the content of teaching, the school timetables and the organization of national examinations. The central body responsible for education in Greece is the National Ministry of Education for the Regions. This Ministry is advised on curriculum matters by the Centre for Educational Studies and Inservice Training (KEME).

State primary and secondary education in Greece is free, and compulsory from the ages of 6 to 15. This comprises primary education (*domotico*) for six years and a further three years of secondary education (*gymnasio*). In practice many students start school when they are less than 6. Children aged between 3 and 5 are provided for in two types of publicly-funded service: either kindergartens, provided mainly by central government, or pre-primary schools (*nipiagogion*), provided by the Ministry of Education. Children in the first three years of primary schooling have 20 hours' teaching a week, increasing to 24–26 for the next three years. Because of a shortage of school buildings, many schools operate a shift system, with the first shift of children attending from 8.00–12.00 and the second for four hours in the afternoon.

Secondary education comprises the *gymnasia* and the *lykeia*. The gymnasium (first cycle of secondary education) lasts three years and is compulsory for students who have graduated from the six-year primary education system; there are no entrance exams. On graduation students are awarded the *apolitirio gymnasiou* (gymnasium diploma)

Holders of the *apolitirio gymnasiou* may enter the *lykeia* without taking any further examinations. This cycle lasts three years and is non-compulsory. It is possible to study this cycle on a part-time basis; this route takes four years. On graduation, students are awarded the *apolitirioi* or *ptychio lykeiou* (*lykeio* diploma or certificate).

There are four types of *lykeia*:

- *Genika Lykeia* (General Lykeia).
- *Technika-Epaggelmatika Lykeia* – TEL (Technical Vocational Lykeia).
- *Eniaia Polikladika Lykeia* – EPL (Unified Multidisciplinary Lykeia).
- *Klassika Lykeia* (Classical Lykeia).

In years one and two, all students follow the same course of study, and attendance at classes is compulsory. During the third and final year of the full-time *Lykeia*, students follow a common course of general interest subjects amounting to ten hours per week, and receive about 20 hours of teaching in one of their *desmes* (specialist subjects taught in preparatory streams which students may select themselves). Upon successful completion, students may enter higher education institutions or seek employment.

In addition to the government-funded state education system, there are several private schools in Greece. Information about these can be obtained from Embassy offices or from the Greek Ministry of Education and Culture. There are also a number of international schools based in and around Athens. Many follow a UK or French curriculum and examination procedure. The majority are fee-paying, although there are a number of international scholarships available.

Special education

Children with special learning needs are generally catered for in special classes in mainstream schools, and as far as possible all children with special needs are given an individual integration plan which outlines their special educational requirements and how they may best be met. Greek education authorities have long recognized that total integration or segregation is often not the best option and that more often, children reach their full potential when greater emphasis is placed on each child's unique needs, rather than relying on a single plan for all children with special needs.

Administration

The Greek government is heavily involved in educational decision-making at all levels, and it has set up numerous national academies and institutions to oversee educational developments in practice. At the same time, particularly since the early 1980s, it has encouraged and facilitated much greater freedom and autonomy for individual institutions to decide upon their own organization's priorities.

Finance

State education in Greece is funded entirely by the government. The main aspects funded nationally are teachers' salaries, school buildings and equipment. Locally based teams of inspectors report to central government in Athens on progress and requirements in local areas. In some cases financial subsidies are awarded to private schools. In addition, the latter also receive income from several private sources including private citizens and professional associations. Some grants are available for students in non-compulsory education and interest-free study loans are available.

VOCATIONAL EDUCATION SYSTEM

Vocational education above secondary level is public and free in Greece. Tuition fees only are covered, not travel and living expenses, although government scholarships are available.

Most vocational training in Greece takes place in Technical Education Schools (TES), Technical Education Institutes (TEIs) and in OAED (Organization for the Employment of the Workforce) training schools. The TES aims to disseminate technical and vocational knowledge and cultivate skills enabling students to practise a given occupation successfully. Entry to a TES is open to holders of the *apolitirio gymnasiou*, to students from any type of general, technical or unified multidisciplinary *lykeia* and to final year students of the latter who have not received a diploma or certificate since they have not completed one or more subjects in their last year.

The TEIs are tertiary colleges, which in Greece means post-18. Courses there last seven or eight semesters (a semester is half a year), including one semester for work experience. Entry to a TEI is by public examination. There are 11 TEIs throughout Greece. Each TEI has six faculties:

- graphic arts and design;
- administration and economy;
- health and caring professions;
- technology application;
- food technology and nutrition;
- agricultural technology.

SELETE is the Technical Teachers Training College in Athens. It plays a major role in enhancing the status of and access to vocational education in Athens. SELETE is government funded. It is located on the same campus as a secondary school where SELETE teacher trainees do school practice. Older school pupils are encouraged to use SELETE laboratories and workshops and receive work experience in a variety of technical skills including TV repair and maintenance, motor mechanics, electrical installation and new technology. In this way students can gain practical experience of technical skills in preparation for further full-time study or employment. There are no sandwich courses in Greece, although some jobs call for one year's practical training before going into a job full-time.

The development of a modular approach to vocational training programmes is high on both the political and educational agendas in Greece. Increased flexibility in the pattern and delivery of vocational training has become of prime importance in the entire vocational education system. Nowadays much greater emphasis is placed on continuing training of the workforce; as a result Greece has increased the numbers of its workforce in training dramatically since the mid 1980s, mainly in the textiles and metal-forming industries. The Ministry of Education is heavily involved in ensuring that continuous improvements are made throughout all industrial sectors. A task force was set up in 1991 to look specifically into apprentice systems, with the primary motive of harmonizing standards with the rest of the EC. In fact, the work in relation to the comparability of vocational training and qualifications between the Member States of the European Community is considered to be of particular importance and usefulness by the Greek authorities. A tremendous effort has been initiated in Greece to update the educational and vocational training system, based on a national dialogue. Elements such as the decentralization of assessment, certification and planning, distance learning, modular training, as well as full-time and part-time vocational studies are intended to be integrated into the vocational training system.

In 1991, the Greek parliament adopted new legislation proposed by the Ministry of Education on Vocational Education and Training (VET). This framework legislation is based on proposals by an *ad hoc* committee aimed at modernizing the VET system and its preparation for the impact of the single European market and Community activities on mutual recognition and comparison of qualifications. The general philosophy underlying the committee's proposals and the new law is designed to complement the existing network of vocational education schools, which operate within the formal education system, with a flexible network of public and private training centres. The new policy is based on three principles. First, *decentralization*: emphasis is placed on decentralizing delivery. The current system, although it has an extensive school network, cannot maintain the same quality of training throughout the country. Certification is time-based which means that there are no national qualification standards. A diploma awarded by an under-staffed and under-equipped school in the countryside has the same face value as diplomas awarded by schools in Athens, Thessalonika or Saloniki, where the training resources and conditions are considerably better.

Therefore, proposals have been agreed to decentralize assessment and certification, in the context of a national competence-based qualification system.

Second, *an active role for the social partners*: the new law required a consensus among the social partners in the planning, assessment and certification of training and on the training of trainers. This has resulted in training curricula that are much more occupation-specific and are also more compatible with the skills needed in the labour market.

Third, *flexibility*: in accordance with European trends, flexibility in training provision and delivery has been emphasized. The new VET system provides accredited training to a whole range of targeted groups (school students, graduates, employers and employees) through a flexible extensive network of training units (both public and private), delivering initial, basic, further and continuing training and retraining in a variety of ways, for example, modular, distance, part-time, open and block training.

In 1991, the Federation of Greek Industries gave its support to initial and continuing vocational training, arguing that such expenditure is a productive investment. The Federation is cooperating with the Greek General Confederation of Labour in order to create a framework for vocational training. The Federation of Greek Industries has suggested an increase of employers' contributions for vocational training from 0.2 per cent to 0.45 per cent, that is an increase of six to seven billion drachma per year. Taking into account that the European Social Fund subsidizes vocational training programmes by up to 75 per cent, the funds made available are increased to 25 billion drachmas. The Federation of Greek Industries has already taken the following measures in regard to vocational education and training:

- a federation for Industrial and Vocational Training was established in 1980 to train workers. To meet the set goals an Institute for Industrial and Vocational Training was established in 1981;
- an Institute for Business Administration was set up in 1989 for training managers;
- the Federation is actively involved in promoting summer jobs and placements in industry for students.

National vocational education and training system

Act 2009 of 2 October 1992 has established a National Vocational Education and Training System (NVETS) which aims to:

- organize, develop and provide vocational training;
- provide the official certification of vocational training;
- coordinate vocational training with the education system;

- develop all kinds of national or community programmes of vocational education and training.

The NVETS follows the current needs of the labour market, the economic and social conditions in the country at national and local levels and scientific and technological developments. It is being formulated and developed in cooperation with the social partners, with all private and public bodies, both Greek and international, and more specifically with the European Community bodies.

The 'Organization for Vocational Education and Training' has been established under the same Act. It is based in Athens and has the following aims:

- the organization and operation of the public Institutes for Vocational Training (IVTs) under the authority of the Ministries of National Education and Religious Affairs;
- the supervision of private IVTs;
- accomplishing the goals of the NVETS.

Its tasks include the following:

- to submit proposals to the Ministries of National Education and Religious Affairs outlining guidelines, planning and programming of the policy on vocational education and training;
- to recognize and certify professions corresponding to the education and training provided by the IVT in accordance with the state and the needs of the Greek labour market, taking into account the current situation in the EC;
- to certify the titles conferred by other Greek bodies involved in vocational education and training;
- to recognize the equivalence of degrees awarded abroad and to provide the necessary information relating to the recognition of rights and certificates and to other requirements for access to regulated professions;
- to define the professional rights of all levels of vocational education and training covered by this law in collaboration with the competent Ministry and social partners;
- to coordinate activities and make recommendations to the Ministries of National Education and Religious Affairs on issues relating to specialization in secondary technical/vocational education and vocational training;
- to define the specifications and grant approval for programmes of formal vocational training provided by other bodies not supervised by the Ministries of National Education and Religous Affairs;
- to take care of programmes relating to the training of vocational

education trainers under the authority of the Ministries of National Education and Religious Affairs.

On 1 September 1992, 15 IVTs began operating on a trial basis. Actual operation commenced on 1 January 1993.

Higher education

Students who wish to enter higher education in Greece after receipt of the *apolitirio lykeiou* sit general entrance examinations which are held each year in June. For certain subjects at higher education level, specialist examinations are also sat as a condition of entry. Even if a candidate passes all his or her examinations, this does not imply automatic acceptance at a higher education institution. Greece applies a quota policy throughout the higher education system, and candidate entry into higher education – up to fulfilment of the quota – is decided on the basis of their marks in the school certificate (*titlo scholikis chrisis*) and their stated preference with regard to the department in which they wish to enrol. As well as traditional institutions offering higher education in a variety of disciplines Greece also has a number of special colleges which provide higher education courses in music, art, drama, television, film, religion, etc.

Adult education

A number of adult education courses exist in Greece both to enable employed adults to keep up to date in their specific occupation, and to provide unemployed adults with the opportunity to retrain in new skill areas and to enhance their employment prospects, while simultaneously increasing their leisure interests. Athens is home to the majority of adult education centres in Greece; rural areas and some of the smaller Greek islands are less well served, although a number of educational cooperatives have been established in the last few years. In order to combat long-term unemployment and to give Greece a confident position in the EC, the government is encouraging all employers to pay much greater heed to the training of their workforce than they have in the past. The government's vocational training financial incentives have been targeted at two main groups: workers in dying industries for retraining purposes, and to economically-deprived areas for rejuvenation programmes.

ECONOMIC FEATURES

The capital city, Athens, has a population of over three million. Few other cities in Greece have populations of over 100,000. Those that do include Piraeus, Patras and Thessaloniki. Because of high unemployment in Greece, it is very difficult for any other EC national to secure anything other than seasonal or temporary work in the tourist industry. Greece's financial position and financial relationship with the EC have been badly strained since the 1980s, when Brussels made the country large loans that were never repaid. Increasingly, the Greek government is moving towards greater privatization, as it is coming under pressure from Brussels to rebuild the economy if it is to keep up with the rest of Europe.

Strike action has been a major feature of economic life in Greece since the mid-1980s, largely as a result of new legislation which seeks to reduce the 1.4 billion social security debt by increasing employee contributions towards pensions and health care. Also, as a result of wage curbs, increases in public utility charges and rises in the price of consumer products, the purchasing power of most Greeks has fallen by about 20 per cent since the beginning of 1990.

Special measures for the unemployed

Since 1990 a special programme has been in force for redundant workers. All employees who are made redundant have the following options:

- *vocational retraining*: persons choosing this option receive a special subsidy amounting to the average of the last monthly wages earned (maximum of Dra 200,000) for a period of 12 months following the termination of the employment. At the same time, these persons select and attend one of the training programmes of the National Manpower Employment Organization (OAED);
- *self-employment*: dismissed persons starting up their own enterprises may receive 12 months special allowance in a lump sum;
- *regular unemployment benefit*.

Subsidies to regular employment from 1992

Since 1992, wage-cost subsidies have been available for newly-created jobs in the private sector, on the condition that there have been no dismissals in the enterprise in the previous three months. Employers (private enterprises, local government enterprises and cooperatives) who employ unemployed persons in new jobs (lasting for at least 16 months) receive a subsidy, for a period of one year, amounting to Dra 2000/day for persons aged 25 years and older and Dra 2200/day for under 25 year-olds. Priority is given to specific target groups:

- employees who have been dismissed from 'problematic' firms (ie, certain firms in the public sector) and who attend a retraining programme: Dra 2500/day for persons aged 18–55 years and Dra 2700/day those aged 56–60 years;

- persons who are employed in areas which are in decline such as Lavrion, Kozani, Evia, Thebes and Ahaia: Dra 2500/day for those aged 18–55 years and Dra 2700/day for those aged 56–60 years;
- inhabitants of Pontos in the former USSR, of Greek origin, returning to Greece: Dra 2400/day;
- employees having completed higher education or a university degree: Dra 2500/day;
- employees in enterprises in frontier regions: Dra 2200/day;
- employees in enterprises in frontier regions in the manufacturing, crafts or mining sectors: Dra 2400/day;
- employees with disabilities: Dra 2600/day.

Financial support for enterprise start-ups

Since January 1992, financial support has been available for 18–50 year olds who set up their own enterprises. The new entrepreneurs receive a subsidy of Dra 350,000 (in services and commerce) and Dra 450,000 (in manufacturing). Persons who have been dismissed from 'problematic' firms and who attend a retraining course receive Dra 450,000 and Dra 550,000 respectively. Persons aged between 25 and 50 years must have been unemployed for at least one year to receive the subsidy.

FINDING EMPLOYMENT

EC nationals have the right to live and work in Greece without a work permit. A full EC passport is required. EC nationals are free to enter Greece for up to three months to look for work or to set up in business. If a stay of longer than three months is intended then a residence permit (*adia diamonis*) is required. A temporary permit is issued in the case of employment lasting over three months but less than 12. Permits are issued for six months in the first instance, and then renewed for a five-year period. To apply for a residence permit outside Athens, contact the local police station. In Athens, registration is through the Aliens Department Office. Before leaving for Greece it is important to contact a Greek Consulate Office (located in all Member States) to check on the up-to-date situation concerning residence permits and on any further documentation that may be required.

EC nationals working in Greece have the same rights as Greek nationals with regard to pay, working conditions, access to housing, vocational education and training, social security and trade union membership.

EC nationals have free access to the services of the Greek employment service. The Manpower Employment Organization – *Organisimos*

Apasholisseos Ergatikou Dynamikou (OAED) is the national job centre, and the address of local offices can be found in telephone directories (*tilephonikos odigos*). OAED's head office also has a European Employment Service.

With very few exceptions, private employment agencies are forbidden by law in Greece. Those which are allowed to operate are called *Idiotika Grafia Apasholisis* and are listed under that heading in the Greek Yellow Pages, *Chryssos Odigos*.

Many national newspapers carry job advertisements. Major newspapers include *Ta Nea* (particularly Wednesdays), *Eleftheros Typos, Eleftherotypia* and *Apogevmatini*. These all carry job pages. However, it must also be remembered that word of mouth is still a very important medium for job-hunting in Greece. Information on employers in Greece is very difficult to obtain outside the country, and using personal contacts is the most effective way of gaining employment. An English newspaper, *Athens News*, also carries job advertisements. Chambers of Commerce in Greece are a possible source of company information.

Speculative applications are common. The CV and covering letter should usually be written in Greek. In general, at graduate level, employers look for a Master's degree, since a first degree is not generally considered enough.

Works councils are compulsory for companies with more than 50 employees, or 20 if there is no trade union. Legal minimum wages are set under the General Collective Labour Agreement (GLCA) for most sectors. The normal working week is 40 hours. Overtime and Sunday working is restricted. Annual leave entitlement is a minimum of four weeks after one year of service. There are also 11 days statutory public holiday.

INFORMATION POINTS

Education and training

Ministry of National Education and Religion
396 Mesogeion Street
Athens

Pedagogical Institute (PI)
Mesogeion 396
15341 Ag. Paraskevi

SELETE
(Technical and Vocational Teacher Training Institute)
Attikas Amarousion
Athens

Task Force
PO Box 70017/16610 Glyfada
Attiki

Ypourgio Pedias & Politismou
Metropoleos Street 15
10 185 Athens

Employment

Athens News
Lekka Street 23–25
105 62 Athens

British Council
Filikis Etairias 17
Kolonaki Sg
106 73 Athens

British Embassy
1 Ploutarchou Street
106 75 Athens

British Hellenic Chamber of
Commerce
Vas Sofias Street 25
Athens

Emborika & Viomichanika
Epimelitino Athinon (EBEA)
Akadimias 7–9
106 71 Athens

OAED
EURES (SEDOC)
(Manpower Employment
Organization)
(Organismos Apasholisseos
Ergatikou Dynamikou, OAED)
Ethnikis
Antistasis 8
166 10 A.Kalamaki

Ypourgio Ergassias (Ministry of
Labour International Relations
Service)
Tmima Diethon Scheseon
Piraeus Street
101 82 Athens

Ypourgio Ikonomikon (Ministry of
Finance)
Tmima Diethon Scheseon
Sina Street 2–4
101 84 Athens

Ypourgio Pedias & Poiltismou
(Greek Ministry of Education and
Culture)
Metropoleos Street 15
10 185 Athens

European Information Centres

Alexandroupolis
Eommex-Alexandroupolis
Euro Info Centre
Miaouli 15
68100 Alexandroupolis

Athens
Chambre de Commerce et
d'Industrie d'Athenes
Euro Info Centre
7 Akadimias Street
10671 Athens

Hellenic Organization of Small and
Medium size Industries and
Handicrafts
(Eommex) – Euro Info Centre
Xenias Street 16
11528 Athens

Panhellenic Exporters Association
Euro Info Centre
Kratinou 11
10552 Athens

Ioannina
Chamber of Ioannina
Euro Info Centre
X. Trikoupi & 14 O. Poutetsi St
45332 Ioannina

Iráklion
Chamber of Iráklion
Euro Info Centre
9 Koronaeou Street
71202 Iráklion – Crete

Kavala
Chamber of Kavala
Euro Info Centre
50 Omonias
65302 Kavala

Larissa
Eommex – Larissa
Euro Info Centre
Marinou Antipa & Kouma Street
41222 Larissa

Mytilini
Eommex – Mytilini
Euro Info Centre
Iktinou 2
Pl. Kyprion Agoniston
81100 Mytilini

Patras
Eommex – Patras
Euro Info Centre
21 Aratou Street
26221 Patras

Pirée
Chambre de Commerce et
d'Industrie du Pirée
Euro Info Centre
1 Rue Loudovicou
Place Roosevelt
18531 Pirée

Thessaloniki
Association of Industries of
Northern Greece
Euro Info Centre
Morihovou Square 1
54625 Thessaloniki

Volos
Association of Industries in Thessaly
and in Central Greece
Euro Info Centre
4 EI Venizelou Rd
38221 Volos

Chapter 7

Ireland

KEY FACTS

Surface area	70,282 sq km, 27,136 sq miles
Capital	Dublin
Major towns	ports Cork, Dun Laoghaire, Limerick, Waterford
Form of government	democratic republic
Population	(1989 est) 3,734,000, annual growth rate 0.1 per cent
Languages	Irish and English (both official)
Currency	Punt
Exports	livestock, dairy products, Irish whiskey, microelectronic components and assemblies, mining and engineering products, chemicals, tobacco, clothing; tourism is important
Vocational educational institutions	Industrial Training Centres; Vocational Education Colleges
Awarding organization	Joint Certifying Body, comprising FAS – The Training and Employment Authority and the Department of Education
Grants	some means-tested grants available,

	although parental contributions are high
Vocational qualifications	National Craft Certificate; Joint FAS/City and Guild of London Institute Certificates; range of certificates awarded by Pitman, the Royal Society of Arts
Trends/developments	the Job Training Scheme introduced by FAS in 1992 is the most recent development in vocational training linking the world of work and training in a practical way. It focuses on tailor-made training programmes in practical and work-based skills

EDUCATION SYSTEM

There is a strong tradition of respect for education in Ireland, and this is reflected in government spending on the education system, which runs at over 6 per cent of total budget. At any given time, over one-quarter of the population is engaged in full-time study, while evening and part-time courses are also very popular. The academic year generally runs from September/October to May/June. The year is organized into three terms, or less commonly, two semesters.

Compulsory education

The Department of Education is chiefly responsible for administering educational provision, and provides compulsory education for 6–15 year-olds free of charge. In practice many 4- and 5-year-olds attend primary schools on a voluntary basis. Primary schooling for children up to the age of 7 lasts for four hours and 40 minutes a day; the school day for this age group is usually from 9.00 to 13.30. For older children, the school day increases to five hours and 40 minutes and generally finishes between 15.00 and 15.30. The lunchtime break, which can vary in length, is supervised and children generally bring their own food, although schools provide cold meals in some disadvantaged areas. There is no formal system of pre-primary education, except for one pre-primary schooling centre in Dublin and approximately 40 centres for travellers' children.

Secondary education

The intermediate certificate is taken at age 15 or 16, and marks the end of compulsory education. After this, students can go on to study towards the leaving certificate which is awarded after a further two years of full-time study, enter a full time training programme or enter employment. It is a state examination, and although no particular subjects are compulsory, students must sit the leaving certificate in at least five subjects. In practice, most pupils take seven subjects. There are higher and ordinary level papers in all subjects. The higher papers cover much the same grounds as the ordinary, but with greater depth and in more detail. Over 30 subjects are available at leaving certificate level.

Special education

The system of special classes in mainstream schools is the most usual method of integrating children with special needs into the education system in Ireland. It is compulsory for children with special needs to attend school from age 6 to 15. At 15 they may transfer to further full-time education or into a vocational training course. As well as special units within mainstream schools, a number of residential schools have also been built to cater for children whose needs are served best in such a setting.

Administration

The Department of Education, based in Dublin, administers the national education system. It cooperates closely with the Catholic church and in particular with church schools. It is responsible for deciding upon curricular aims and content as well as on examination procedure and award systems. As well as the Department of Education's role, the Irish government has set up a number of other organizations to oversee education policy and practice, including the Higher Education Authority (HEA) which is a state body with both executive and advisory functions in relation to the support and development of higher education by the state. Vocational Education Committees (VECs) are responsible for the administration of technical and continuing education within particular regions, and they are responsible for administering grants to the regional technical colleges.

Finance

Compulsory education is free, although parents may be asked to contribute to the cost of textbooks and other school equipment. Means-tested grants, loans and scholarhips are available for students in post-compulsory education, but again parents are often asked to contribute, sometimes in quite large amounts. Most state subsidization of universities and other third-level colleges (all forms of education provided in or by institutions of higher education) is directed through the Department of Education via the Higher Education Authority.

VOCATIONAL EDUCATION SYSTEM

Most training for young people is organized by the state Training and Employment Authority, FAS, CERT (Council for Education, Recruitment and Training for the Hotel, Catering and Tourism Industry) and ACOT (Council for Development in Agriculture). Some training is also provided through Community Training Workshops and Travellers' Training Centres.

At the national level responsibility for apprenticeship education and training lies with FAS in collaboration with the Department of Education. It is possible that some quite substantive changes may take place in the near future; the coalition government has created a new Department of Enterprise and Employment, with a commitment to establish a Comprehensive National Training Scheme and a National Education and Training Certification Board. Legislation is due to be introduced in late 1993 to fund a new Apprenticeship Scheme. In practical terms the education and training of apprentices involves a partnership between industry, FAS and the Vocational Education Authorities. Industry employs the apprentices and provides on-the-job training and experience; FAS is the registration authority. The Vocational Education Committees provide structured theoretical and practical programmes to equip an apprentice with knowledge and understanding of the basic principles which underpin his or her craft.

FAS runs a wide range of training programmes in Ireland, both for retraining workers in new skills and helping younger school-leavers to acquire industrial skills. FAS also provides an advisory service for industry and education, and operates an overseas training organization called the Irish Labour Training Services (ILTS) which negotiates training contracts and exchanges with other European countries. As well as FAS activities, a number of UK awarding bodies such as RSA and Pitman provide for vocational training routes.

Vocational Education Committees (VECs) are responsible for the administration of technical and continuing education within particular regions. They are also responsible for the administration of state grants to:

- Regional Technical Colleges (RTCs);
- the Dublin Institute of Technology (DIT);

• other specified colleges.

The National Council for Educational Awards (NCEA) is the body that validates the majority of courses provided by the Regional Technical Colleges. The RTCs provide a comprehensive range of courses, including second-level craft and apprenticeship programmes and third-level certificates, diplomas and degree courses.

The Dublin Institute of Technology and other colleges within the vocational sector also provide education which is oriented towards vocational and professional needs. The provision of third-level part-time evening courses is a major function of the DIT. There is intense competition for the limited number of university, RTC and other third-level places, which are allocated on the basis of leaving certificate results, so the standard of students accepted for full-time further and higher education is high, which in turn contributes to a high standard of degree, diploma and certificate holders.

Higher education

Higher education in Ireland is funded mainly by the state. Courses of higher education are provided at over 40 institutions. Entry into university is reserved largely for students in possession of the final secondary school leaving examination – the leaving certificate – which is awarded after a two- or three-year course at second level school. For most pupils, the leaving certificate is studied for immediately after the intermediate certificate has been awarded at 16, that is, from 16 to 18 or 19. Students sit the leaving certificate in at least five subjects, although most pupils take seven. There are higher and ordinary level papers in all subjects. For admission to non-university higher education, the leaving certificate is again the main entry qualification. However, other entry qualifications include GCSE A-levels, senior trade certificates of the Department of Education, and the National University of Ireland (NUI) matriculation examination.

In higher education students are given a number of options both as to the subjects they study and the length of time they wish to stay. For example, within a given field of study, a student could progress from completing a one-year certificate to the second year of a national certificate programme; from that, on to the third year of a national diploma programme; and from there on to a degree.

Adult education

The adult education system in Ireland is quite well established, particularly the sophisticated network of distance learning programmes which was developed in the early 1980s. The take-up rate is increasing annually, and the range of subjects available has more than doubled since the distance learning programme started.

Various forms of post-school training exist outside the formal further and higher education routes. These include programmes sponsored by FAS and administered by local training schemes. It is also possible to sit the leaving certificate outside of the school system. The government is increasing its commitment to vocational education for adults and in turn, encouraging employers to consider on-going training and inservice training for all staff, and to make the most of the training opportunities available in their local areas.

ECONOMIC FEATURES

The Irish economy is mixed, with private ownership the norm, but the state operates much of the transport, communications, electriciy, gas, health and education services. Since the late 1980s the government has moved to privatize some of these activities, and this process is continuing. Successive governments, irrespective of the political party or coalition in power, have diligently wooed overseas companies to set up in Ireland, as part of a strategy for providing jobs and boosting the economy.

Programme for Economic and Social Progress

The success of the Programme for National Recovery in terms of economic expansion and employment growth confirmed the desirability of continuing the process of national consensus between the government and both sides of industry.

The Programme for Economic and Social Progress (PESP) provides a strategic framework for the 1990s with specific proposals for the early years of the decade on:

- macroeconomic stability policies, geared to low inflation, low interest rates and reduction of the national debt; and
- a programme of fundamental structural reforms, especially a continuation of the radical tax reform begun under the Programme for National Recovery, a major assault on long-term unemployment and a restructuring of social welfare, the health services, education and housing.

Features of the Programme which are of particular relevance to the labour market include:

- a comprehensive agreement on pay and conditions between the Irish Congress of Trade Unions (ICTU) and employers' organizations;
- the creation of 20,000 new jobs for each year of the programme in

manufacturing and international services (ie, an average employment growth of 2 per cent per annum);

- the introduction of an integrated, area-based response to break the cycle of long-term unemployment by way of a progression through the various education, training and work-scheme initiatives;
- the introduction of a standards-based apprenticeship system and the creation of an additional 3000 places for apprentices over the period of the programme.

Key objectives

In agreeing the terms of a successor programme (PESP), the government accepted the ICTU's proposal to adopt a long-term strategy for national development over the next decade. Key objectives are:

- sustained economic growth and the generation of greater income to produce a narrowing of the gap in living standards between Ireland and the rest of the European Community, based on increased enterprise, efficiency and competitiveness and maintaining a low-inflation economy;
- a substantial increase in employment;
- a major assault on long-term unemployment;
- the development of greater social rights within health, education, social welfare and housing services;
- the promotion of collective and individual social responsibility in relation to discharge of tax liabilities, fair conduct in business dealings, sensible treatment of the environment and reasonable use of the public services; and
- the development of worker participation, women's rights and consumers' rights.

Employment Subsidy Scheme and Job Training Scheme

The Employment Subsidy Scheme and Job Training Scheme were formulated in November 1991 against the background of a worsening employment situation in Ireland. The two initiatives are aimed at increasing the level of training and reducing unemployment.

Employment Subsidy Scheme

This scheme is open to employers in the private sector, commercial state bodies and voluntary bodies which can provide additional permanent full-time employment opportunities. The normal wage for the job must be paid and jobs subsidized under the scheme must be additional. The target for the scheme is 15,000 jobs and it is now operational.

Job Training Scheme

This scheme is a work-based training programme by employers in cooperation with the National Training Authority (FAS). Under the scheme,
the world of work and training will be linked in a positive manner.
Trainees taken on by employers will follow a structured and supervised
programme of training in a work-based setting, tailored to their individual needs. Employers will in turn gain by having a trained pool of labour
on which to call and from the long-term spin-off benefits this will bring
in terms of improved company performance.

The Job Training Scheme will be administered by FAS which will also
award certificates to successful trainees. Trainees will receive normal
FAS allowances from the employer.

To make use of the scheme, an employer must be able to provide
training on a full-time basis. The employer must also complete an
application incorporating a training specification which sets out the
aims, the training outline, the duration, the approach and the proposed
system for assessment and certification.

The participation target for the scheme is 10,000 trainees. This target
is considered to be ambitious as the scheme is thought to be a major new
departure which represents an important opportunity to make a major
breakthrough in encouraging training by employers, as this is generally
believed to be an area which could be expanded upon.

Principal incentives to industry

For over 30 years tax relief has been a key incentive for manufacturing
industry in Ireland. It is an incentive which has been maintained by
successive governments – an endorsement of their support for private
enterprises and the growth of industry.

Tax relief has formed an important part of the total package of
generous grants and incentives which has helped Irish industry to expand
and grow. It has also encouraged many other firms to invest in Ireland –
over 1000 overseas companies have set up in Ireland since 1960.

In 1980 the Irish government introduced a new tax incentive for manufacturing and certain non-manufacturing industry as well as certain non-
manufacturing activities – a 10 per cent rate of corporation tax to the
year 2000. In 1990 the incentive was extended for a further ten years to
2010, showing a continuing support for private enterprise and an appre-
ciation of its need for certainty about the continuing availability of this
incentive.

The reduced rate of corporation tax at just 10 per cent applies in
respect of income arising in the period from January 1, 1981 to
December 31, 2010 from the sale of goods manufactured in Ireland.
'Manufacture' is widely defined: in addition to conventional manufac-

turing, a range of other activities can qualify, including certain design and planning services, computer services and income of trading houses.

The 10 per cent rate applies only to manufacturing profits. Passive income is liable to corporation tax at the full rate of 40 per cent. However, this usually can be mitigated with appropriate planning. The following are some examples:

- income on certain government securities is exempt from tax;
- dividends and interest paid by US corporations (including Irish branches of US banks) are exempt from Irish tax where the recipient is non-Irish resident (eg, it could be the Irish branch of a foreign company);
- where certain conditions are met, relief is granted from corporation tax in respect of dividends from non-resident subsidiaries.

Many overseas companies carry out manufacturing activities in Ireland and qualify for the 10 per cent rate. These include over 300 US companies, almost 200 UK companies and over 150 German companies. Many of these companies are large multinationals.

Companies that locate in the Shannon area may qualify for the 10 per cent rate in respect of all their activities provided they contribute to the use of Shannon Airport and are export-orientated. Their range of activities is not confined to manufacturing and financial services.

FINDING EMPLOYMENT

EC nationals have the right to live and work in Ireland without a work permit, but a full EC passport is essential; a visitor's passport or excursion document is not sufficient. EC nationals working in Ireland have the same rights as Irish citizens with regard to pay, working conditions, access to housing, vocational education and training, social security and trade union membership.

EC nationals have free access to the services of the Irish employment service, called The Employment and Training Authority, and usually referred to by its abbreviation, FAS – *Foras Aiseanna Saothair*. FAS offices can be found across the country. To find the address of the nearest office, look in the Irish equivalent of Yellow Pages, *Golden Pages*.

All private employment agencies must be registered and licensed by the Department of Labour, which holds a list of all employment agencies in Ireland. They are listed in *Golden Pages* under Employment Agencies. Large public reference libraries in other EC countries often carry copies of *Golden Pages*.

Major national newspapers in Ireland tend to have a particular day for job advertisements, for example, *The Irish Independent* (Thursdays) and

The Irish Times (Fridays). Chambers of Commerce also hold information about large employers.

The normal working week is between 38 and 42 hours; the legal maximum is 48 hours per week or nine hours per day. Annual leave entitlement is a minimum of 15 days for most employees in the private sector after eight months' service. In practice many employees receive more than the minimum. There is no minimum wage legislation, although there are legally binding collective wage agreements in many sectors. There is no legal requirement for companies to have works councils.

INFORMATION POINTS

Education and training

Department of Education
Marlborough Street
Dublin 1

Higher Education Authority
21 Fitzwilliam Square
Dublin 2

The Training and Employment
Authority (FAS)
27–33 Upper Baggot Street
Dublin 4

EOLAS
(The Irish Science and Technology
Agency)
Glasnevin
Dublin 9

Regional offices of EOLAS:

Donegal and North West Regional
Office
Finisklin Industrial Estate
Sligo

East Regional Office
Glasnevin
Dublin 9

Midlands Regional Office
Auburn
Dublin Road
Athlone

Mid West Regional Office
The Granary
Michael Street
Limerick

North East Regional Office
Finnabair Industrial Park
Dundalk
Co. Louth

Shannon Laboratory
Shannon Town Centre
Shannon
Co. Clare

South East Regional Office
Georges Street
Waterford

South West Regional Centre
Industry House
Rossa Avenue
Bishoptown
Cork

West Regional Office
Industrial Estate
Mervue
Galway

IDA Ireland
(Industrial Development Authority
of Ireland)
Head Office
Wilton Park House
Wilton Place
Dublin 2

Employment

The Chamber of Commerce of
Ireland
22 Merrion Square
Dublin 2

Department of Social Welfare
College Road
Sligo

Department of Labour
Davitt House
65a Adelaide Road
Dublin 2

Irish Congress of Trade Unions
(ICTU)
Head Office
19 Raglan Road
Dublin 4

The Revenue Commissioners
Dublin Castle
Dublin 2

European Information Centres

Cork
Cork Chamber of Commerce
European Business Information
Centre
67 South Mall
Cork

Dublin
Irish Export Board/Coras Trachtala
European Business Information
Centre
Merrion Hall
PO Box 203
Strand Road – Sandymount
Dublin 4

Galway
Galway Chamber of Commerce and
Industry
Euro Info Centre
Hynes Building
St Augustine Street
Galway

Limerick
Shannon Free Airport Development
Company
European Business Information
Centre
The Granary
Michael Street
Limerick

Sligo
Sligo Chamber of Commerce
European Business Information
Centre
16 Quay Street
Sligo

Waterford
Waterford Chamber of Commerce
European Business Information
Centre
CTT Office
Industrial Estate
Cork Road
Waterford

Chapter 8

Italy

KEY FACTS

Surface area	301,300 sq km, 116,332 sq miles
Capital	Rome
Major towns	Milan, Turin; ports Naples, Genoa, Palermo, Bari, Catania, Trieste
Form of government	democratic republic
Population	(1990 est) 57,657,000, annual growth rate 0.1 per cent
Languages	Italian, German, French
Currency	Lira
Exports	wine (world's largest producer), fruit, vegetables, textiles (Europe's largest silk producer), leather goods, motor vehicles, electrical goods, chemicals, marble (Carrara), sulphur, mercury, iron, steel
Vocational educational institutions	State Vocational Schools; Vocational Training Centres
Awarding organizations	Ministry of Public Education; Regional Authorities; Ministry of Labour (Local Employment Sections)
Grants	means-tested grants are available in

	some regions for a range of vocational subjects; some scholarships available
Vocational qualifications	Vocational Skills Diploma; Certificate of Vocational Skills; Statement of Vocational Skills
Trends/developments	renewed emphasis on the development of generic skills coupled with changes in the design of training involving a shift from the traditional trainer-centred form to a learner-centred form of provision.

EDUCATION SYSTEM

The state education system is mainly controlled by the Ministry of Public Education, although regions are responsible for vocational training centres. Private schemes parallel both systems, conforming to national norms. Teachers are state employees and syllabuses are determined centrally. Tuition is free and most higher education students receive a grant (economic background and marks obtained at examinations are a prerequisite for qualifying for a grant). Attendance at school is compulsory from 6 to 14 and most younger children attend pre-primary schools. Pre-school education is provided in both state and private nursery schools and although attendance is optional, over 90 per cent attend full-time, six days a week. Pre-primary education is provided by central government, local authorities, or private organizations, both religious and lay, which receive public funding.

Compulsory education

The school year runs from early September to the end of June, with two short holidays of a fortnight at Christmas, one week at Easter and four public holidays. In most private schools pupils attend from 8.00 to 16.00 five days a week, with an optional half day on Saturday. In state schools, with the exception of full-time experimental schools, the timetable for primary schools is 8.30 – 12.30 six days a week and for middle schools, 8.30 – 1.30 three times a week and 8.30 – 12.30 three times a week.

Primary education is from 6 to 11 in two cycles, with a two-year general curriculum concentrating on the 3Rs, and continuing in a three-year phase in which subject learning is begun. The fifth year ends with an examination for the primary school certificate (*licenza elementare*) which admits pupils to the middle school, where three years are spent studying for the intermediate school certificate (*licenza di scuola media*). Twenty-six hours a week must be given to certain compulsory subjects: religious instruction, Italian, history, civics and geography, mathematics, nature study and elementary science, a foreign language, art education and physical education. In some areas, an option of an extra ten hours covers extra studies and out-of-school activities. Repeat examinations for pupils in difficulties have recently been replaced by 'support courses' during the latter half of the year.

Special education

Most children with special learning needs are integrated into mainstream schools in Italy. They must attend school for at least eight years, from 6 to 14, after which they can continue in full-time education until they are 18, or enter a vocational training programme.

Administration

Two ministries have the main responsibility for education and culture in Italy: the Ministry of Public Instruction (MPI) which controls antiquities, fine arts, libraries and archives, and the Ministry of Labour which is responsible for some vocational training.

Syllabuses are organized centrally and all teachers and educational administrators are state servants employed by the MPI. Private institutions must satisfy MPI standards if their students are to have legally valid qualifications. The MPI central inspectorate review school activities, including those of schools in the private sector.

Regional school boards are responsible for school buildings and qualifying courses for secondary school teachers, but their function is mainly consultative. Universities, although in theory autonomous, are partly controlled by the MPI.

Finance

Public sector expenditure on education represents just under 5 per cent of GNP. Apart from the MPI, other government departments contribute to education about one sixth of the MPI expenditure, while regions and districts contribute over a quarter of the amount spent by central government. Some means-tested grants and scholarships are available for students undertaking courses after compulsory education has finished. For certain courses, students who obtain higher marks in examinations or assessments may qualify for larger grants or other forms of financial assistance.

VOCATIONAL EDUCATION SYSTEM

Post-compulsory education

Pupils who have obtained the intermediate school certificate (*licenza di scuola media*) have access to one of five types of specialized schools (higher secondary schools). In some categories entry is also possible with the elementary certificate plus an entrance examination. These establishments cater mainly for 14- to 19-year-olds, and those completing the course successfully qualify for university entry; the vocational diplomas also provide access to the intermediate professions. The five types of school are as follows.

1. *Grammar schools* are either classical or scientific; Latin is required to enter the former. After five years' study in a broadly based curriculum, students sit for the *maturità* (higher secondary certificate), consisting of two written examinations and an oral examination in two subjects. In both types of school, the five-year course is divided into two cycles, with nine subjects in the first and 11 in the second; the balance differs, 2+3 for the classical type and 1+4 for the scientific.

2. *Artistic education* either in artistic grammar schools or art institutes; the former have four-year courses, divided after a common two years, into two sections: either preparation for study in the Academy of Fine Arts or the architecture faculty, or for art teaching in intermediate schools.

3. *Teacher training*, non-advanced, is in two categories: (a) teacher training schools, which provide a three-year diploma course for nursery school teachers. Entry is via the intermediate certificate. During the second and third years a parallel apprenticeship course is followed in the nursery school(s) attached to the training school. (b) Teacher training schools, which provide a four-year diploma course for elementary school teachers, also qualifying successful candidates for entry to teacher training courses at university, and to any faculty, after successful completion of one year at higher secondary school. The two latter years of the course include teaching practice.

4. *Technical institutes* provide five-year vocational courses in eight basic types: agriculture, commerce, surveying, maritime, industry, women's studies, business and tourism; concentrating on academic subjects in the first two years and more vocational subjects later. The teaching timetable is intensive, averaging 40 hours a week.

5. *Vocational institutes* provide vocational training (more practical than in technical institutes) mainly via two- or three-year courses, exceptionally four- or five-year (to gain university access), under six types: agriculture, industry, maritime, commerce, hotel and tourism,

and women's studies. The diploma leads to employment, but also entitles the holder to continue his or her studies at a technical institute, after an entry examination.

Once they have left school young workers can continue their studies part-time, usually at evening classes, or as registered apprentices. (Employers with apprentices in training do not pay social insurance contributions.) Many large firms, for example, Fiat and Olivetti, do their own training. For new employees coming out of the public education system these firms start from scratch, ie, they do not build upon the foundations laid in school. Workers are entitled to paid leave to sit examinations, and to work timetables which enable them to attend night school. The curriculum there is similar to the day programme, involving four hours' study on five nights a week, plus Saturday morning attendance, for up to six years. The qualification obtainable is the *diploma di maturita*.

Vocational education

Vocational education and training in Italy is still very much in the developmental stage, as a result of which there are many systems in operation. While this broadens the choice for young people leaving school, it also mitigates against any attempt to provide a cohesive and standardized route into many industrial, commercial and professional sectors. Italy also suffers from many dichotomies, between the Ministry of Education and Ministry of Labour, between state and industry/commerce, and between employers and employees. No recognizable 'dual system' is in operation, and very little interchange occurs between representatives of industry and education. One exception to this, however, is ISFOL (*Istituto per lo Sviluppo della Formazione Professionale dei Lavoratori*), financed from public funds, and operating in collaboration with the Ministry of Labour and Regional Administrations in the development of vocational and professional training through the promotion of research, innovation, professional enrichment and research into the demands and needs of the world of work. It provides technical assistance in training programmes and projects, experimentation in teaching and multi-media programmes, and policy papers on teaching and training methodologies and work orientation.

In Italy much vocational education and training is carried out by the higher technical schools (*Istituti Professionali* and *Istituto Tecnici*). In the *Istituto Professionali* courses start at age 14 and run for a minimum of two and a maximum of five years. Vocational education is also carried out locally by the Regions or Communes and also by private authorities operating with public funds. After reaching the end of compulsory education at 15/16, young people may either:

- take up full-time employment of some sort (usually unskilled);
- take up an apprenticeship involving 40 hours per week of which eight must be specifically for training;
- register at a locally run *Centri di Formazione Professionale* (CFP) or at a state *Istituto Professionale*; or
- register at a traditional higher secondary school, that is, a *Liceo Classico* (humanities), *Liceo Scientifico* (Sciences) or a *Liceo Artistico* (arts), leading on to work or to university.

In essence, therefore, vocational education (other than that provided by firms to their own employees) takes place in one of two ways;

- in the state (Ministry of Education) *Istituto Professionali* with a two-year exit point, or in some, the option of a further three years. *Istituto Tecnici*, on the other hand, offer five-year courses only, leading to a *Diploma di Maturita Tecnica* which is fully recognized for the purposes of employment in all industrial and commercial fields or for university entrance in any faculty; or
- in the locally run (Ministry of Labour) CFPs where *corsi di formazione professionale* (vocational training courses) in various sectors are offered: fashion, agriculture and food, commerce and business, interior design, social work and health care.

Higher education

Qualifications for admission to higher education
A *maturità* examination, based on a five-year course, entitles students to enrol in all university courses and can be taken in the the following fields:

- science (*diploma di maturità scientifico*)
- technical (*diploma di maturità tecnico*)
- classics, languages or literature (*diploma di maturità classico*)
- art (*diploma di maturità artistico*)
- teaching (*diploma di maturità magistrale*)

The *maturità* allows entrance to any Italian university, although some universities are very selective and take only students with the best results. Eventually every student will find a place but it may not be exactly where he or she wishes it to be, such as in one of the universities enjoying an excellent reputation like those in Milan, Padua, Pisa etc. There is, incidentally, an International University at Perugia at which foreign students already at university in their own country may spend a year learning Italian language and literature.

There are not very many private (ie, non-state) universities in Italy but of these the most well known are:

Milan:
Libera Universita Cattolica del S. Cuore
Libera Istituto Universitario di lingue Moderne
Universita L. Bocconi – Commerce and Economics
Politecnico Milano

Naples:
Istituto Universitario Navale

Urbino:
Libera Universita

Turin:
Polytecnico

Venice:
Istituto Universitario di Architettura

Rome:
Libera Universita Internazionale degli studi sociali

In addition, there are 39 state universities. University courses last for a minimum of four and a maximum of six years, the latter in, for example, medicine and architecture, and there is a growing number of two- to three-year diploma courses. Over one million students enrol annually for higher education, mainly in universities or university institutes, or in private universities, which may receive some state aid on application. Although there is no formal arrangement for part-time study, only one in three students attend regularly and the rest combine work and study. The *laurea* is the main educational qualification in Italian universities; they also confer various types of diploma as final educational qualifications, though on a much smaller scale.

Teacher training

As noted above, pre-primary and elementary school teachers are qualified at non-advanced level; they constitute about one third of the teaching force. Teachers in post-compulsory education must have a university degree, and pass either a further examination and practical tests or else achieve a post based on both academic and teaching qualifications (the procedure has been altered repeatedly recently). Candidates must then pass successfully a year of teaching apprenticeship.

University teaching staff are recruited by national competition based on academic qualifications, a written examination and an interview. Researchers are recruited on the basis of their academic qualifications and an interview.

Entry to all faculties requires the possession of the secondary school leaving certificate diploma: the *maturità*, obtainable after five years of higher secondary school. Numbers are not otherwise limited in the state sector. In theory, private universities must have the same entrance standards, but in practice, can be selective and restrict intake.

Qualification examinations are held at the end of each year and the results of each course entered on the degree certificate. After all courses have been successfully completed, the student submits a thesis and is examined on it orally by 11 faculty members. The final degree standard is based on their marks, and the title 'Doctor' is awarded. Apart from the rare diploma courses noted before, there are post-graduate degree courses. As courses may be repeated and thesis preparation has no time limit, degrees are rarely awarded after the minimum period.

Adult education

All workers are entitled to have 150 hours of paid leave (over a three-year period) to complete their compulsory schooling, that is, to obtain the *licenza di suola media*. Such education is provided through evening classes in state schools and can also be attended by unemployed persons. Educational qualifications are required not only for entry to training opportunities and employment, but to obtain certain civic rights and to undertake certain civic duties. There is a growing number of opportunities for adults to retrain, attend language classes or use correspondence or open learning courses.

ECONOMIC FEATURES

Italy is well placed in the European Community. Northern Italy is at the heart of Europe from a communications viewpoint, and Milan has one of the busiest international airports in Europe. It also boasts an enviable amount of motorways, 31 in all, covering some 6000 kilometres, of which 1000 are toll-free.

Italy is in the process of economic reform and new economic policy changes are being introduced. Since the late 1980s it has been running Europe's largest current account deficit in relation to its national output. In a bid to cut the budget deficit, the government has announced the privatization of one of Italy's biggest banks, the *Credito Italiano*, and a large engineering company, the turbine builder *Nouvo Pignone*. Increased privatization is rapidly becoming the government's response to intense pressure from *Confindustria*, the powerful employers' association, to begin selling off the swollen state sector. Changes are also being planned to Italy's investment taxation regime as part of the government's economic package.

There are several sorts of taxes in Italy, such as IVA (*Imposta sul*

Valore Aggiunto) equivalent to VAT in the UK, and IRPEF (*Imposta sul Reddito delle Persone Fisiche*) and ILOR (*Imposta Locale sui Reditti*) which are somewhat equivalent to British capital gains tax, but are applicable only to real estate.

Employment promotion measures

In 1991, new legislation introduced a number of changes to labour regulations, in particular:

- reform of the Wage Compensation Fund, known as the CIG;
- new mobility lists;
- reform of recruitment procedures.

Reform of the Wage Compensation Fund

Regulations governing special wage compensation and special unemployment benefits have been modified in relation to the conditions governing eligibility for these allowances and the granting procedure to be followed.

Special wage compensation intervention is subject to an evaluation of the programme of recovery of full company operations submitted by the company and the length of the programme. This intervention is reserved for companies which employ more than 15 employees (including apprentices and persons with a training-cum-work contract) during the six-month period prior to the application for compensation. The application must include the programme which the company intends to implement and possible provisions to remedy the social implications.

Another important aspect of the 1991 modifications is the duration of the intervention. It may not, under any circumstances, exceed 48 months, including extensions. This period will be reduced to 18 months for wage compensations during the time that a company is filing a petition for bankruptcy, and to 12 months in the case of a company crisis. Shorter periods are foreseen for enterprises in the building and agricultural sectors.

In the framework of the contributions which are payable by the enterprises, the amount of contribution due will be doubled at the end of the 24 months so as to discourage extensions. Furthermore, the regulation foresees that, for each production unit, the special wage compensation payments may not exceed a total of 36 months in a five-year period, irrespective of the reasons for which the grant has been awarded.

Enterprises which employed workers on the basis of a solidarity contract to avoid redundancies are subject to limitations when appealing to the CIG. Enterprises which applied for ordinary intervention for production units, may not apply for the special compensation payment for these units for the same period. Major limitations are thus envisaged to limit the use which is made of the CIG and to restore the ClG's original role, ie, intervention in situations of temporary and occasional surplus manpower.

An important new aspect has also been introduced by Law 223/91 as regards surplus workers whom enterprises, which benefit from the special intervention of the CIG, will be unable to re-employ. In this case, companies can initiate redundancy procedures which involve an initial written notification to the company's union representatives. The letter must indicate the number of persons involved, technical reasons for the redundancy, when it will take effect, etc.

After obtaining the union's approval, the enterprise may place surplus workers and managers on the mobility list by informing each of them in writing and by sending a list to the regional labour office of all the workers who have been made redundant.

Workers who are made redundant are chosen according to the regulations laid down in the collective agreements or the following criteria:

- family dependants;
- length of service;
- worker's qualifications in relation to the technical requirements associated with production and administration.

For each worker who has been made redundant, the enterprise is required to pay 30 monthly payments to the responsible service of the National Social Insurance Institute (INPS). The payments are equal to six times the initial monthly redundancy payment received by the worker concerned. This amount is halved in the case of a union agreement. Reductions on payments are foreseen for enterprises which offer permanent employment contracts to workers whom they have put on the mobility lists.

New mobility lists

Based on directives issued by the Ministry of Labour, after consultation with the Central Employment Commission and technical analysis conducted by the Employment Agency, the regional employment office draws up a complete mobility list of workers who have been made redundant. This list is based on files containing information which is useful for their re-integration, such as: occupation, preference for a job which is different from the previous position, willingness to accept a job in another area, etc.

A mobility list will therefore include the following:

- workers who have been made redundant due to over-staffing and through the above-mentioned procedure by the following employers:

- enterprises which receive special wage compensation for structural staff surpluses;
- enterprises which are subject to regulations when filing a petition for bankruptcy;
- enterprises which employ more than 15 wage earners and which, because of reduction or transformation of activities, intend to dismiss at least five employees, in the space of 120 days, in one or more production units, in the same area of a given province;

• workers receiving special unemployment benefit;
• workers employed in companies of the Industrial Management and Participation Group (*Gestione e Partecipazioni industriali* – GEPI) and the Sardinian Initiatives (*Iniziative Sardegna Spa.* – INSAR) who were receiving a CIG allowance on 31 December 1988 and were made redundant according to a reduced procedure.

Workers who have been made redundant are entitled to an allowance for a maximum period of 12 months; for 40-year-olds the period is 24 months and for 50-year-olds it is 36 months. This allowance covers 100 per cent of the special wage compensation for the first 12 months; between the thirteenth and thirty-sixth months it covers 80 per cent. It must therefore be linked to the worker's length of service.

Workers are removed from the mobility list in the following cases:

• refusal to attend a vocational training course;
• refusal to accept work which is professionally equivalent, similar or corresponding to at least 90 per cent of the former job;
• refusal to participate in works of public utility;
• failure to inform the INPS branch concerned of the work carried out;
• when employed on a full-time permanent contract;
• when having made use of the possibility of capitalizing the total amount of redundancy allowance;
• when the period for which payments and allowances are awarded has expired.

Reform of recruitment procedures

New recruitment procedures have been introduced to make it easier for employers to recruit redundant workers. Employers who offer newly redundant workers employment on the basis of a fixed-term contract (maximum of one year) benefit from reduced social security contributions which are usually reserved for apprenticeship contracts. These reductions can be extended by 12 months if the contract is altered to a permanent employment contract. If full-time permanent jobs are offered by employers then, for a period of 12 months, employers will receive monthly compensation equal to 50 per cent of the redundancy payment that the worker would have been awarded

Positive action to support female entrepreneurship

On 25 February 1992, Law 215 was passed in order to foster basic equality and equal opportunities for men and women in economic and entrepreneurial activities. The main objectives are to:

- foster the creation and development of female entrepreneurship, particularly in the most innovative fields of the various productive sectors;
- promote entrepreneurial training and to further the professionalism of businesswomen;
- encourage (also in financial terms) enterprises with predominantly female personnel;
- develop women's knowledge of the running and management of family businesses.

The following organizations are envisaged as benefiting from the new law:

- cooperatives and companies in which at least 60 per cent of the workforce is female;
- companies where at least two-thirds of the shares are owned by women;
- individual enterprises which are managed by women;
- enterprises, associations, companies, organizations promoting entrepreneurship, those with combined public and private funds, training centres and professional associations which promote business training courses or enterprise creation, or consultancy services and technical and managerial support services which have 70 per cent of their total employment and training places or services reserved for women.

National fund

A national fund has been established for the development of female entrepreneurship with a financial allocation of LIT 30 billion for 1992–94, spread evenly over the period. Through the fund, the first three types of enterprises mentioned above may obtain the following facilities:

- financing of up to 50 per cent of expenditure for installation and equipment;
- reimbursement of up to 30 per cent of the costs incurred for the purchase of services which, amongst other things, are intended for increased productivity, for reorganization, the transfer of technology and the development of quality systems.

These subsidies can be increased to 60 per cent and 40 per cent respectively if the beneficiaries work in the areas as specified in EC regulation no. 2052/88 (Abruzzo, Apulia, Basilicata, Calabria, Campania, Molise, Sardinia and Sicily and in the territories hit by industrial decline). Furthermore, the last category of enterprises listed above may be reimbursed by the fund for up to 50 per cent of the costs incurred for activities undertaken.

The regulation also provides for financial facilities through credit institutions and banks of no more than LIT 300 million for a maximum of five years. The interest rate will be 50 per cent of the rate that applies in the sector to which the beneficiary company belongs. The interest rate may be reduced to 40 per cent in relation to the going rate for enterprises which are active in the south of the country, as indicated above.

Committee for Female Entrepreneurship
The Committee for Female Entrepreneurship has been set up by the Ministry of Industry and Trade. It consists of the Ministers of Industry and Trade, of Labour and Social Security, of Agriculture and Forestry, and of Finance, or their delegates. Furthermore, credit institutions are also represented, as are representative organizations for the cooperative sector, for small industry, trade, handicrafts, agriculture, tourism and services.

The members of the Committee are nominated by decree by the Minister of Industry and Trade and sit on the Committee for a period of three years. This Committee is responsible for the management and general programming of the subsidies which are laid down by regulation (Law 215/92) and promotes studies, research and information on female entrepreneurship. A sum of LIT 500 million has been set aside for the implementation of the Committee's activities.

FINDING EMPLOYMENT

EC nationals have the right to live and work in Italy without a work permit. A full EC passport is required and a visitor's passport or excursion document is not sufficient. Visitors intending to look for employment must obtain a worker's registration card (*libretto di lavoro*), which is kept by the employer, or during periods of unemployment, by the job centre, the *Ufficio di Collocamento Manodopera* (UCM). Visitors searching for employment must report to the local police headquarters (*questura*) within seven days of arrival to apply for a residence permit (*permesso di soggiorno*), which enables the holder to stay in Italy and look for work for three months. After three months a second application has to be made for an extension to the *permesso di soggiorno*, and renewals are made through the local police. All renewals must be made on special document paper (*carta bollata*) which can be purchased from most tobacconists (*tabaccherie*).

EC nationals working in Italy have the same rights as Italian nationals with regard to pay, working conditions, access to housing, vocational education and training, social security and trade union membership. They also have free access to the Italian Employment Service, the UCM, whose offices are located throughout Italy; the address of the nearest office can be found in the Italian equivalent of the Yellow Pages, *Pagine Gialle*, listed under *Ufficio di Collocamento*.

Private employment agencies are not allowed to operate in Italy; however, a chain of employment bureaux called *Il Recruit Shop* opened in Milan in 1991. They are particularly useful for graduates with vocational qualifications, mainly business, economics and computing. The same graduates are also in demand from employers at the new national graduate recruitment fair organized in Milan by the *Association des Etats Generaux des Etudiants d'Europe* (AEGEE).

Advertisements in the national press are the main source of vacancies for graduates and holders of specific vocational diplomas or certificates. Major newspapers carry jobs pages on certain days of the week, and there are specific periodicals for many public sector vacancies. For example, teaching and other public sector jobs are advertised in the *Gazette Ufficiale*. Major newspapers include *Corrière Della Sera* (Fridays) and *La Repubblica*. Useful regional newspapers include *La Stampa* in Piedmont, *Il Giornale* in Milan and the Rome-based *Il Messaggero*. The major financial dailies include *Il Sole/24 Ore* and *Italia Oggi*, and they too carry job pages. In addition, there are two fortnightly English-language journals which cover the Rome area and carry job pages: *Wanted in Rome* and *Metropolitan*. Another source of possible contacts in Rome, Florence, Milan and Bologna is the English Yellow Pages, and in some areas, other EC telephone directories are available in the public library or at UCM offices.

Workers in companies with more than 15 employees are entitled to form works councils if they wish. Most employment sectors have their own legal minimum wage which is set annually. All employees receive an extra month's wage ('the thirteenth month') in December. Some sectors divide the annual salary into 14, 15 or 16 payments.

The standard working week is 40 hours with a legal maximum of 48 hours. Overtime, which cannot be demanded of any employee, is paid at a rate of 130–150 per cent of the normal hourly rate. In practice, however, many unions have agreed bans on overtime. Annual leave ranges from 25 to 30 days depending on length of service. In addition, there are also ten days' statutory public holiday.

Family links form a major part of job-hunting in Italy, and many companies have little interest in recruiting non-Italian workers. A common way into employment in Italy is via a placement scheme whilst studying.

Application forms are not commonly used in recruitment and selection. CVs should be in Italian and be accompanied by a covering letter and names and addresses of referees.

INFORMATION POINTS

Education and training

Consorzio Europea per la
Formazione Professionale
Corso Italia 7
20122 Milan

ISFOL
Direttore Generale
via B. Eustachio 8
00161 Rome

Dipartimento per il Co-ordinamento
delle Politiche Comunitarie
Presidenza del Consiglio dei Ministri
Via del Tritone 142
00187 Rome

Ministero della Pubblica Istuzione
Viale Trastevere 76/A
00153 Rome

Employment

British Chamber of Commerce for
Italy
Via Agnello 8
20121 Milan

British Embassy
Via XX Settembre 80a
00187 Rome

European Information Centres

Ascoli Piceno
Camera di Commercio IAA di Ascoli
Piceno
Eurosportello Azienda Speziale
Via Luigi Mercantini 23/25
63100 Ascoli Piceno

Bologna
Associazione Degli Industriali Della
Provincia di Bologna
Eurosportello Assindustria Bologna
Via San Domenico, 4
40124 Bologna

Bari
Istituto Finanziario Regionale
Pugliese Finpuglia
Euro Info Centre
Via Lenin 2
70125 Bari

Brescia
Rete Artigianato
Comitato Coordinamento
Confederazioni Artigiane
Eurosportello
Via Cipro 1
25124 Brescia

Cagliari
CCIAA Cagliari
Eurosportello
Viale Diaz 221
C/o Centro Servizi Promozionali per
le Imprese
09126 Cagliari

Catania
Camera di Commercio Industria
Artigianato e Agricoltura di Catania
Eurosportello
Via Cappuccini 2
95123 Catania

Chieti
Eurosportello della Camera di
Commercio Industria Agricoltura e
Artigianato
Piazza GB Vico 3
66100 Chieti

Firenze
Consorzio Eurosportello –
Confesercenti
Eurosportello
Piazza Pier Vettori 8/10
50143 Firenze

Promofirenze
Eurosportello
Via Faenza 111
50123 Firenze

Genova
Camera di Commercio di Genova
Eurosportello
Torre WTC-San Benigno
Via de Marini 1, III p
16149 Genova

Isernia
CCIAA Isernia
Euro Info Centre
Corso Risorgimento 302
86170 Isernia

Milano
Associazione Industriale Lombarda
Euro Info Centre
Via Pantano 9
20122 Milano

Camera di Commercio Industria
Artgianato e Agricoltura di Milano
Eurosportello
Via Delle Orsole 4/B
20123 Milano

Napoli
Camera di Commercio Industria
Artgianato e Agricoltura di Napoli
Eurosportello
Corso Meridionale 58
80143 Napoli

Palermo
ME. SVIL. SPA
Euro Info Centre
Via R. Wagner 5
90109 Palermo

Perugia
Centro Regionale Commercio Estero
c/o Camera di Commercio di Perugia
Euro Info Centre
Via Cacciatori delle Alpi 40
06100 Perugia

Pesaro
Associazione 'Compagnia delle
Opere'
Eurosportello – Eurocdo
Via V Rossi 2
61100 Pesaro

Ravenna
CCIAA Ravenna
Euro Info Centre
Viale LC Farini 14
48100 Ravenna

Roma
Confederazione Generale Dell'
Agricoltura Italiana
Euro Info Centre
Corso Vittorio Emanuele 101
00186 Roma

Confederazione Generale Italiana
del Commercio e del Turismo
Euro Info Centre
Piazza GG Belli 2
00153 Roma

Institute for Development of
Southern Italy (IASM)
Euro Info Centre
Viale M Pilsudski 124
00197 Roma

Unioncamere/Mondimpresa/Cerved
Eurosportello
Piazza Sallustio 21
00187 Roma

Torino
Camera di Commercio Industria
Artigianato e Agricoltura di Torino
Euro Info Centre
Via San Francesco da Paola 24
10123 Torino

Federpiemonte
Euro Info Centre
Corso Stati Uniti 38
10128 Torino

Udine
Camera di Commercio IAA
Euro Info Centre
Via Morpurgo 4
33100 Udine

Venezia Mestre
Centro Estero delle Camere di
Commercio del Veneto
Euro Info Centre
Via Menestrina 94
30172 Venezia Mestre

Vicenza
Associazione Industriali della
Provincia di Vicenza
Euro Info Centre
Piazza Castello 3
36100 Vicenza

Chapter 9

Luxembourg

KEY FACTS

Surface area	2,586 sq km, 998 sq miles
Capital	Luxembourg
Form of government	liberal democracy
Population	(1990 est) 369,000, annual growth rate 0 per cent
Languages	French (official); local Letzeburgesch; German
Currency	Luxembourg franc
Exports	Luxembourg is economically linked to Belgium; exports pharmaceuticals and synthetic textiles; international banking is important
Vocational educational institutions	on-and-off-the-job training is undertaken jointly by employing organizations and colleges of technology
Awarding organization	Ministry of National Education and Professional Chambers
Grants	grants available to undertake full-time vocational training in Luxembourg, and scholarships to study in other EC countries

Vocational qualifications	Vocational Training Certificate (CAP); Vocational and Technical Training Certificate (CATP)
Trends/developments	trend towards increased cooperation between employing firms and educational institutions in the development and forecasting of vocational training requirements

EDUCATION SYSTEM

State education is free in Luxembourg and is administered by the *Ministère de l'Education Nationale* (National Ministry of Education). Private education is also administered by the same government department. All sectors of education are governed by regulations and directives drawn up and administered by the National Ministry of Education.

Compulsory education

Compulsory education begins at age 5 and finishes at age 15, but in practice most attend both pre- and post-compulsory education. Both pre-primary and primary schooling are generally in the same school and follow the same hours: 8.00 – 11.30 and 14.00 – 16.30 three days a week, and 8 – 11.30 on three days a week including Saturday. In addition, *foyers de jours* provide full-time care for 3-year-olds and outside school hours care for 4-year-olds at pre-primary schooling. Full-time secondary education can be extended to age 19 at a grammar school.

A school leaving certificate is obtained after seven years of consecutive full-time study at a *lycée classique*, a *lycée technique* or at the European School in Luxembourg. A *lycée classique* provides general education, whereas a *lycée technique* leads to a technical school leaving certificate which is more vocationally oriented. For the general school leaving certificate pupils take final examinations in seven or eight subjects. The certificate is awarded in six specialities:

- arts and humanities;
- sciences;
- natural sciences;
- law and economics;
- art;
- music.

For the technical school leaving certificate, there are 11 compulsory subjects. Admission to institutions of higher education for students with diplomas from a *lycée technique* is usually limited. However, it does provide a direct path to the *Institut Supérieur de Technologie de Luxembourg* (IST), which provides a complete, professionally oriented education. All examinations are state examinations, and even pupils from private schools sit the state examinations. There are no periods of continuous assessment, so little weight is attached to academic achievements which fall outside the final examination results.

There are a number of international schools and European schools in Luxembourg which follow a UK or French curriculum and examination procedure. Because of the high number of foreigners living in Luxembourg, language education is widely available and offered free of charge to recent immigrants.

Special education

Schools and centres are provided for children with motor and sensory disabilities as well as for children and young people with special learning needs. Compulsory education lasts for ten years from age 5-15 and can be extended on a part-time voluntary basis up to age 19 if a student wishes. Provision is made for pre-school children with special needs to attend local centres attached to primary schools.

Administration

The National Ministry of Education is responsible for educational administration in both the public and private sectors. It also has overall responsibility for educational policy and planning in the public sector. In the higher education system, all institutions are public; there are no church-affiliated or private institutions.

Finance

State education is free in Luxembourg. Grants and interest-free loans are available for students who wish to pursue their education beyond compulsory education. Some scholarships are available for certain subjects.

VOCATIONAL EDUCATION SYSTEM

In-company training programmes and colleges of technology feature highly in the Luxembourg system of vocational education and training. Vocational training certificates (CAP), and vocational and technical training certificates (CATP), are two of the most common vocational qualifications which are administered by Professional Chambers under the auspices of the Ministry of National Education.

Luxembourg has four colleges for advanced vocational training. To gain admission to a full-time vocational course, one of the following diplomas must be obtained:

- a secondary or a designated technical secondary school leaving certificate;
- a foreign secondary school leaving certificate recognized as equivalent;
- a technical diploma.

The first two diplomas make one eligible for admission to university. Vocational education is provided through apprenticeships which can be either full- or part-time joint courses between employers and colleges of technology. Qualifications are awarded by Professional Chambers or by the Ministry of Education.

Higher education

The diplomas most commonly held by persons admitted to higher education are secondary school diplomas, which are usually obtained after seven consecutive years at a *lycée classique*, a *lycée technique* or at the European School in Luxembourg. The different diplomas are:

- the secondary school leaving certificate of the *lycée classique* (*diplôme de fin d'études secondaires*)
- the technical secondary school leaving certificate of the *lycée technique* (*diplôme de fin d'études secondaires techniques*)

Higher education in Luxembourg is quite limited and the majority of students go to Belgium, Germany or France to study at this level. In Luxembourg, any EC national who wishes to pursue a higher education course must take one of the following routes:

- a first-year university course (*Cours Universitaire*) at the *Centre Universitaire de Luxembourg* (CUL). Enrolment at the CUL is compulsory for future teachers at higher secondary school level;
- non-university courses of three years at:
  - the *Institut Supérieur de Technologie de Luxembourg* (IST), and
  - the *Institut Supérieur d'Études et de Recherches Pédagogiques de Luxembourg* (ISERP);
- non-university courses of two years at:
  - the *Institut de Formation pour Educateurs et Moniteurs de Luxembourg* (IFEM), and
  - the *Cycle Court de Luxembourg* (CC).

Non-univeristy institutions offer advanced vocational training for technical engineers, primary and elementary school teachers and bankers.

Adult education

The relative paucity of formal higher education places in Luxembourg is countered by the well-established training programmes conducted by several employing organizations. Adult continuing education is considered important by all four parties: employers, employees, training centres and the government; as a result, numerous training programmes have been developed. Adult exchange programmes to other EC countries are also well developed, and day or block release for students to attend relevant courses is considered an important element in employees' career packages.

ECONOMIC FEATURES

The Grand Duchy of Luxembourg, with an area of 998 square miles and no more than 50 miles from north to south and 35 from west to east, is one of the smallest states of Europe. But, for several reasons, it has an importance out of proportion to its size. Situated between Belgium, France and Germany, it lies on routes between the Rhine and the Paris basin and between the Belgian ports and central Europe. The basis of its prosperity in the past has been the large iron and steel industry.

Of the population of nearly 400,000 about two-thirds live either in the capital, Luxembourg, (70,000) or in the iron and steel districts. Today, many large international corporations have permanent establishments in Luxembourg including Western Tobacco, Cargolux, Goodyear and Du Pont.

A chief industrial source of revenue is still iron and steel production, based on the ore mines of the south-west and yielding the highest per capita quota of any country in the world. Over 90 per cent of the steel is exported. Lack of coal for the furnaces has long necessitated economic union with other countries: in the 19th century, within the German customs union; and since 1921, with Belgium. Currently a member of the Benelux Union, the European Coal and Steel Community (administered from Luxembourg City) and the EC, Luxembourg, because of its iron and steel industry, has an important place alongside larger nations on the continent.

Agriculture, forestry and wine production give work to about a quarter of the population. The estates are generally small- to medium-sized and cultivated by their owners, rented farms being exceptional. Vine growing, for the production of both still and sparkling wines, is concentrated along the slopes of the Moselle Valley bordering Germany. While some of the forest is state owned and some in private hands, most of it is owned by the village communes and used to meet local requirements.

Luxembourg has the highest immigration rate in the EC and the lowest birth rate in the world. High immigration will continue since the country depends upon a well-qualified labour force. Foreigners account for a massive 43 per cent of the labour force. The main groups are EC citizens, some of whom are staff of the European Community. There are also some 14,000 third-country nationals from the USA, Cape Verde and Iran. There are two main categories of immigrant labour: first, those employed in the tertiary sector and the international civil service and, second, those who work in the industrial, agricultural and service sectors. Public service employment is restricted in the civil service, local government and nationalized industries to those holding Luxembourg nationality. Manual posts in state employment are open to all.

Because of its reliance on foreign workers and the need to maintain a well-qualified labour force, the Luxembourg government has introduced measures to ensure that the children of immigrants have the same opportunities as Luxembourg children when they enter employment. In addition, government policy to deal with the lack of qualifications amongst certain groups is worthy of note. Language education and skills training is modified and targeted to suit the needs of the relatively disadvantaged groups such as recently arrived immigrants.

Employment promotion measures

Reform of legislation on disabled workers
Legislation concerning disabled workers was radically amended in 1991. The Law both reforms and coordinates legislation relating to the vocational rehabilitation, integration and reintegration of disabled workers, adapting it to reflect changing ideas which are widely acknowledged as determining the attitude of society on this question.

The Law takes a number of fundamental principles into account. Rehabilitation should in fact be regarded as a continuous process, from the onset of the disability through to vocational integration under the best possible personal and working conditions. Furthermore, it is vital to determine right from the start the extent of the physical and learning capabilities of the person concerned, in order to decide which occupations would be most suitable. Once the disabled worker has received occupational guidance, training should be provided which would offer him or her the best possible job appropriate to his or her skills. The next step is to guarantee employment opportunities for disabled workers by employing, on a compulsory basis, a certain percentage of disabled workers within firms, with the state setting an example. Finally, it is customary for disabled workers to receive a salary in line with their working skills and abilities.

It is clear that the disabled worker must be given assistance throughout the various stages by an effective permanent body charged with the task of providing advice and help in finding employment or in re-entering the labour market. In particular, the Minister of Labour considers it important to ensure that the services specialized in placing disabled workers operate within the bodies responsible for placing other workers, and that the services are readily accessible to those interested. In order to operate at peak efficiency, the services responsible for placing disabled persons must therefore be part of the normal employment services and must maintain close links with them. The personnel deployed must have had special training and possibly some work experience on the open labour market.

The amendments to the law can be summarized as follows:

- to integrate the present service responsible for placement and occupational re-training of disabled workers as a service within the Employment Administration;
- to broaden the legal field of application to those people with learning handicaps or persons with a sensory handicap;
- to determine measures to be taken aimed at occupational integration or re-integration of disabled workers;
- to determine, by means of national legislation, the form and content of measures relating to placement, vocational training or re-training courses on adjustment or re-adjustment to work;
- to increase the level of compulsory employment for the benefit of disabled workers in firms and enterprises in the public and private sectors;
- to develop and adapt the scope of the Employment Administration personnel by increasing staffing levels in the service provided for disabled workers through the use of specialized staff;
- to create a legal framework for public aid from which private groups or bodies can benefit.

Voluntary part-time work

The Luxembourg Bill on part-time work was introduced in 1991 and is part of a strategy involving free recourse to part-time work. Its aim is to eliminate obstacles to this type of work, taking into account two areas of concern. In the first place, care must be taken to ensure that employers are not disuaded from offering part-time jobs when there is a real need for such jobs on the labour market. In the second place, the employee who chooses to work part-time must be given sufficient guarantees.

The Bill opts for a plan of action which, without directly and actively encouraging the promotion of part-time work, aims to put an end to the discrimination, both legitimate and effective, which employees who choose this type of work may suffer in comparison with full-time employees. Part-time employees must have a status corresponding to that of full-time employees. Efforts must be made to ensure that part-time work does not lead to the employee being marginalized within the company.

The main points of the Bill can be summarized as follows:

- managing directors of companies are obliged to consult the workers' committee or the employee representatives before creating part-time posts;
- employees of the company concerned, who have expressed the wish to take up or to resume part-time work, are informed first should such jobs become available;
- it is not permitted to dismiss a full-time employee who refuses to do part-time work;
- rules concerning the content of the part-time employment contract;
- the regulation of overtime;
- the rights of part-time employees with regard to salary as well as to determine rights of seniority and to calculate severance pay and the trial period;
- rules concerning representation of part-time employees on employee representation committees.

FINDING EMPLOYMENT

EC nationals have the right to live and work in Luxembourg without a work permit. A full EC passport is essential; a visitor's passport or excursion document is not sufficient. Visitors who intend to work in Luxembourg for more than three months have to register with the local authority, the *Administration Communale*, for an identity card (*carte d'identite*) which is valid for five years and also serves as a residence permit.

EC nationals working in Luxembourg have the same rights as Luxembourg nationals with regard to pay, working conditions, access to housing, vocational education and training, trade union membership and social security arrangements. They also have free access to the services of the Luxembourg government's Employment Service, an office of *l'Administration de L'Emploi*. The address of the nearest office can be found in the telephone directory (*Annuaire Téléphonique*) or the Luxembourg equivalent of the Yellow Pages, *Ligne Bleue*. To remain registered at *l'Administraion de l'Emploi*, jobseekers are required to visit the placement office at least once every fortnight. Private employment agencies are listed under *Agences de Travail* in *Ligne Bleue*.

Major national newspapers in Luxembourg carry jobs pages. They include *Luxemburger Wort* (published in bilingual form), *Republicain Lorrain* and *Tageblatt*. Most job vacancies are advertised in the *Luxemburger Wort* (Saturdays). There is also an English-language weekly newspaper, *Luxembourg News*, which also features job advertisements. Another information source is the *Financial Times* (Friday) which is widely available in Luxembourg.

Although there is no specific graduate recruitment season in Luxembourg, employment prospects are better than in most other EC countries. As it does not have any institutions of its own producing graduates, Luxembourg nationals will have studied abroad and all therefore finish their studies at different times. The country's economy centres on financial services (there are over 170 banks) and the European Community institutions.

Initial job applications usually involve a CV and a handwritten accompanying letter. The CV is shorter than a UK version because hobbies and extra-curricular activities are usually excluded. Application forms are sometimes used and are often filled out at the first interview. The CV, accompanying letter and application form should normally be written in French, unless a job advertisement specifically states otherwise.

The legal maximum working week in Luxembourg is 48 hours, or 10 hours per day. A normal working week is usually about 40 hours. Annual leave entitlement is a minimum of 25 days after three months' service. There is a legal minimum wage that is fixed twice-yearly. Companies with more than 15 employees must have employee representatives, and companies with more than 150 employees must have a works council.

INFORMATION POINTS

Education and training

Ministère de l'Education Nationale
29 rue Aldringen
2926 Luxembourg

Employment

Administration des Contributions et
des Accises (tax)
45 boulevard Roosevelt
2982 Luxembourg

Administration de l'Enregistrement
et des Domaines (customs and excise)
1–3 ave Guillaume
1651 Luxembourg

Accueil des Etrangers (residence
permits)
9 rue Chimay
1333 Luxembourg

Chambre de Commerce du grand
Duché de Luxembourg
7 rue Alcide de Gasperi
2981 Luxembourg

Centre Commun de la Sécurité
Sociale
Offices des Assurances Sociales
125 route d'Esch
1471 Luxembourg

L'Administration de l'Emploi
(government employment service)
38a rue Phillipe II
Boite Postal 23
2010 Luxembourg

European Information Centres

Chambre de Commerce du
Grand-Duché de Luxembourg
Euroguichet
7 rue Alcide de Gasperi
BP 1503
2981 Luxembourg

Chambre des Métiers du
Grand-Duché de Luxembourg
Euroguichet – Luxembourg
41 rue Glesener
1631 Luxembourg

Chapter 10

The Netherlands

KEY FACTS

Surface area	41,863 sq km, 16,163 sq miles
Capital	Amsterdam
Major towns	The Hague (seat of government), Utrecht; chief port Rotterdam
Form of government	constitutional monarchy
Population	(1990 est) 14,864,000, annual growth rate 0.5 per cent
Language	Dutch
Currency	Guilder
Exports	dairy products, flower bulbs, vegetables, electronics, petrochemicals
Vocational educational institutions	in-firm and off-the-job training is jointly organized by vocational schools and industry or trainee workshops; higher education takes place in *Hogescholen*
Awarding organizations	Training Boards
Grants	students in post-compulsory education, or their parents, may apply for means-tested grants; scholarships

	and interest-free loans are also available
Vocational qualifications	apprenticeship certificates; diploma from a Training Board
Trends/developments	several new regional training courses have been developed. Also, improvements in the training-employment relationship have occured under the 'impulse programmes' which have enhanced the tuning of supply (education) and demand (enterprise)

EDUCATION SYSTEM

Children may attend nursery schools from their fourth birthday. Although attendance is voluntary, 95 per cent of 4- and 5-year-olds attend. Nursery schools do not teach children in the strict sense of the word: these schools have play-and-work plans. Since 1985 nursery and primary education has been integrated, thus creating an uninterrupted process of education for 4- to 12-year-olds.

Compulsory education

Education is compulsory for all 6–16-year-olds. Compulsory education is free, apart from contributions to school funds which may be required in private education. From the fifth year of secondary education fees are assessed, based on income and family size. The school year begins in August, with a five-day week the norm.

Primary education

Primary school covers six years (ages 6–12), with a minimum of 1000 teaching hours per year (880 for the first two years). The basic primary school day is 9.00 to 16.00, with a two-hour lunch break; schools are closed on Wednesday afternoons. Since the mid-1980s an increasing number of schools have adopted a 'continuous timetable', which involves a shorter school day with a shorter midday break.

The syllabus includes the basic tools of learning as well as general development subjects. Progress is assessed regularly and repetition of a year is not unknown. The form teacher is responsible for all subjects, but some subjects (physical education, handicraft, religious education, needlework) may be taught by specialist teachers. Pupils in higher classes may learn English, the favoured second language, or sometimes French. In the final year pupils are tested to determine the most suitable type of secondary school.

Secondary education

Admission to secondary schools is gained on the basis of the primary school headteacher's report and the primary school final year's test results. During the first (transitional) year all pupils are reassessed and transferred to a different form of secondary education if necessary.

Secondary education in the Netherlands caters for the 12–18 age range in two main branches: general pre-university education, and vocational pre-work education. To facilitate the movement of pupils between the various kinds of school, two or more different types of school may form a combined institution of vocational and general school; of various levels of general education; or of various types of vocational education.

Senior secondary vocational education lasts a maximum of four years, covering technical subjects and natural sciences; personal and social services and health care; commerce and agriculture. Shorter courses (two or three years full-time) are also available, and practical work in and outside school forms an important part of such courses.

Five types of secondary education can be distinguished: pre-university education (VWO), junior and senior general education (MAVO, HAVO) and junior and senior vocational training (IBO, MBO), of which the latter (MBO) belongs to the higher stage, since it has no direct entry from primary school. All types of schools may be combined in school communities (with one school board and one principal), which may also include types of vocational training.

Pre-university schools (VWO) have a six-year course and prepare pupils for university entrance. The final examination includes seven subjects, which are chosen in the fifth year under certain conditions (Dutch and one modern language obligatory and, as the case may be, Latin and/or Greek).

Senior general schools (HAVO) offer a five-year course and give access to vocational colleges (HBO; non-university higher education). The leaving examination comprises six subjects, which must include Dutch and one foreign language.

Junior general schools (MAVO) have a four-year course. The leaving certificate (six subjects, Dutch and one foreign language obligatory) gives access to senior vocational training (MBO). Many leavers, however, continue in the fourth year of senior general schools (HAVO).

Special education

Special education caters for children requiring educational treatment in various ways: bargees, caravan and showpeople's children, children with learning difficulties and children with specific disabilities (deaf, blind, physically handicapped, etc). Special education is provided at pre-primary, primary and secondary school level, and is compulsory from 6 to 16. In some cases it can be extended for four extra years up to a student's 20th birthday.

Administration

The Ministry of Education and Science has overall responsibility for education and is advised by the Educational Council. The Minister of Agriculture and Fisheries is responsible for agricultural education.

State education is provided by central or local government. The central government inspectorate has an important role in maintaining standards.

Finance

Government expenditure on education amounts to approximately 7.5 per cent of GNP each year. The funding system varies according to the level of education. State pre-primary, primary schools and special schools are provided by the municipalities. The Ministry of Education pays all staff salaries directly, while the remaining costs are reimbursed to the municipalities on the basis of standard amounts per pupil and per schoolroom. Staff salaries of both public and private schools for second-ary education are also directly paid by the Ministry. The remaining current costs of general secondary schools are reimbursed by the Ministry on the basis of standard amounts per school, per unit of space and per student. The expenditures of secondary schools and vocational schools are refunded by the Ministries of Education and of Agriculture on the basis of the expenditure records of each school.

The financing of universities is based on the so-called General Financial Scheme, agreed upon between both public and private establishments and the Ministry and submitted to parliament. Individual universities subsequently receive state funds on the basis of their budgets after these have been approved by the Minister.

Students in post-compulsory education, or their parents, may apply for state grants, the amounts of which depend on the parents' income. In higher education scholarships consist of 60 per cent grant and 40 per cent interest-free loan. The loan must be repaid in ten years, starting not later than in the second year after completion of the study. Parents maintain-ing a full-time student of over 21 years of age receive a child allowance.

Study grants and loans amount to aproximately 4.5 per cent of total government expenditure on education each year.

VOCATIONAL EDUCATION SYSTEM

Junior vocational training (IBO) is provided in courses that last four years. The first two are almost entirely devoted to general subjects and the last two to vocational training. Secondary (or junior) vocational education is provided at the following:

- schools for technical education;
- schools for domestic science/home economics;
- schools for agricultural education;
- schools for education in retail and trades;
- schools for economic and administrative education;
- schools for services and health care education.

In some areas special schools (or departments in schools) cater for pupils who need individual attention owing to learning or behavioural problems.

In most fields the final examination can be taken at various levels (A, B, C), to be chosen, by the pupil, per subject. Usually at least two or three subjects (dependent on the field) must be done at C-level (the highest) for access to senior vocational training.

Senior vocational training (MBO) is open to pupils who have completed either the corresponding junior vocational training, or junior general school. The length of courses varies, up to a maximum of four years, including a practical year. Here too fields can be distinguished: as well as those mentioned under junior vocational training there are at this level socio-pedagogic courses (social work, prison work, some types of counselling, etc) and training for laboratory personnel.

Short senior vocational training programmes cater for 16- to 18-year-olds, who need not have completed their preceding education or training. It provides facilities for vocational training (in various fields) and also for orientation and connecting 'education to work' programmes. The maximum length of these programmes is three years.

Young workers' educational institutes are not schools in either the formal or the material sense: their activities are not concerned with intellectual training as such, but with the development of young people in relation to the actual circumstances in which they live and work. The Dutch government has an on-going support programme in operation which assists these organizations.

The apprenticeship scheme in the Netherlands operates on the lines of the 'dual system' involving one or two days a week at school and the rest of the week in industry or a trainee workshop. The occupations covered range through the technical sectors, caring professions, social and personal services, catering and retail. Apprenticeship schemes are characterized by agreements that apprentices receive general and theoretical vocational training at appropriate institutes and at the same time do the corresponding practical work with their employer. Apprentices have usually completed junior vocational training, but may also come from other types of education.

Higher education

At present two types of higher education exist side by side: vocational colleges or higher professional education (HBO) and university education (WO).

Vocational colleges (HBO) provide courses with a duration of usually three or four years, open to students who have – at the least – completed senior vocational training (MBO) or senior general education (HAVO). HBO is taught at *hogescholen*, of which there are over 90 in the Netherlands. *Hogescholen* provide training for the professions and for middle and top management positions in large- and medium-sized companies as well as in the service sector.

The disciplines within higher professional education at HBO are divided into the following seven sectors:

- *Hoger pedagogisch onderwijs*, HPO (education)
- *Hoger agrarisch onderwijs*, HAO (agriculture)
- *Hoger technisch onderwijs*, HTO (technology)
- *Hoger gezondheidsonderwijs*, HGO (health)
- *Hoger economisch onderwijs*, HEO (administration)
- *Hoger sociaal-agogisch onderwijs*, HSAO (social studies)
- *Hoger kunstonderwijs*, KUO (fine arts).

The main difference between them and the universities (WO) is the emphasis on practical applications in the subject areas. University education requires a certificate of pre-university education, *voorbereidend wetenschappelijk onderwijs*, (VWO), a *middelbaar beroepsonderwijs*, (MBO) (secondary vocational education, intermediate level), or a *hoger algemeen voortgezet onderwijs*, (HAVO) (general secondary education, higher level) for entrance.

In 1982/3 new regulations came into force concerning the duration of studies at higher education level: the first (propaedeutic) examination must be passed after one year and the final (doctoral) examination after a total of four years. Only a limited number of graduates will be allowed to go on to the second stage, which may lead to a doctorate or professional qualification for physicians, dentists, veterinary surgeons and pharmacists.

The Open University (OU) was introduced in 1984 as a type of distance learning for students age 21 and over. It does not have any entrance requirements. Courses are offered in almost 50 subjects and an adequate combination of courses will, if desired, lead to graduation at either vocational college or university level. This means that depending on the number, type and levels of the courses followed, a period of study at the OU leads to a *certificat* (certificate), a *diplomadossier* (diploma file), a diploma or a degree.

Adult education

Most courses which are available in vocational schools can also be taken by adults at day schools or evening schools. Most centres are attached to existing secondary and vocational schools. There are also programmes offered by commercial institutes, leading to similar certificates. Many organizations offer correspondence courses and some provide shortened routes to qualifications through intensive residential courses.

Retraining is provided in state institutes under the Ministry of Social Affairs or with a personal state allowance in other institutes. Private firms may also train their own employees, whether or not in cooperation with training institutes. Since the mid-1980s the government has been actively encouraging employing organizations to introduce on-going staff training programmes.

A number of institutes provide non-certificated courses in hobbies, general interest, and cultural or social development. The majority of these institutes are state aided (Ministry of Well-being, Public Health and Culture), although a growing number are provided by cooperatives and women's training centres.

Post-higher education (PHO) courses are on a smaller scale and of a shorter duration than typical post-doctoral programmes; the aim of PHO courses is not so much to teach a certain profession but to offer continuing education in a specialized area to persons who are already employed. For admission, students must possess a doctoral or HBO diploma. Foreign students may be admitted if they have diplomas or an acceptable period of work experience at a comparable level.

ECONOMIC FEATURES

The Kingdom of the Netherlands covers about 13,600 square miles but this figure is increasing as more and more land is won from the sea. The main occupations are connected with agriculture. Cereals, potatoes and sugar beet are grown on the higher lands of Groningen, Friesland and

Zeeland, whilst on the damp lower ground of Friesland and the provinces of north and south Holland large numbers of cattle are reared, for both meat and dairy products. The bulb fields around Haarlem are a highly productive specialist industry supplying an international market. Fishing is another important occupation and there are many fishing ports along the North Sea coast, notably IJmuiden, Scheveningen and Vlaardingen.

The importance of industry in The Netherlands is increasing. There are coal mines in Limburg, as well as oil fields and natural gas in Drenthe. Philips radio and electrical works, dominating the town of Eindhoven, employs over 35,000 people. Amsterdam and Rotterdam are great commercial cities. Rotterdam, one of the main transit centres for goods passing to and from Central Europe via the Rhine, is the largest port in continental Europe.

Employment incentives

Since 1989 new measures to encourage the employment offices to concentrate more on acquiring vacancies which can be filled by persons who are currently looking for work have been in place. As many jobseekers who are registered at employment offices have few qualifications, this means that employment offices must aim particularly at vacancies for unskilled work, or work for which these people can be trained.

These plans were introduced by the Minister for Social Affairs and Employment in a document outlining priorities for 1993–7. The Cabinet indicates which areas of the Employment Service's policy ought to be changed. The document has triggered talks in the Central Employment Board (CBA) on the subject of the labour market policy to be pursued and the consequent market strategy for the period. Results of these talks will be embodied in the National Multi-year Policy framework 1993–7 which will be drawn up by the CBA.

It has also been proposed that the Employment Service should devote its energies to improving the quality of the services it offers. The target to fill 144,500 vacancies in 1993 must not be increased in 1994. Moreover, there is also a call for extra efforts for three special groups of unemployed persons:

- ethnic minorities;
- unemployed persons who are partially incapable of working;
- the long-term unemployed.

A so-called 'proportional target' applies for the three groups. This means that the employment offices must aim to fill the same proportion of vacancies with members of the target groups as these groups share in the file of registered jobseekers.

Priority given to the newly unemployed is to be determined on a regional basis. The Regional Employment Boards (RBAs) would thus be given the possibility of adapting wage cost subsides and employment integration programmes to regional circumstances.

The Ministry believes that persons who are partially incapable of working, for example, temporarily disabled people, should be helped in their search for work by the employment offices, in close collaboration with the labour experts from the industrial insurance board. For this group of partially disabled persons, the proportional target must be attained by the end of 1996.

Up until the end of 1990, unemployed women constituted a separate target group. The proportional target has virtually been reached for this group. In future, therefore, employment offices must concentrate on those groups of women who nevertheless still hold a weak position on the labour market, ie, those from ethnic minorities, long-term unemployed and partially disabled women. Extra attention must be paid to women who receive unemployment benefit or social assistance (ABW) and who register at the employment office, to prevent their joining the ranks of the long-term unemployed.

In addition to the measuers outlined above, the Minister proposes that from 1993 employment offices should offer training and vocational preparation to 4000 young persons. The target is to allow 4000 young people to participate in training which prepares them for the apprenticeship system. Finally, the Minister expects that the employment offices will help to maintain the levels of influx into the apprenticeship system of 56,000 young persons per year.

FINDING EMPLOYMENT

EC nationals have the right to live and work in The Netherlands without a work permit. A full EC passport is essential; a visitor's passport or excursion document is not sufficient. EC nationals are free to enter The Netherlands for up to three months to look for work or set up in business. Visitors must register with their local aliens administration office (*Vreemdelingenpolite*) within eight days of arrival. No official authorization documents are required to work in The Netherlands unless it is to work for the government. Visitors who intend to stay for over three months must apply for a residence permit (*Verblijfsvergunning*). This can be obtained from the *Vreemdelingenpolitie* with confirmation from an employer that you have a contract for longer than three months.

EC nationals working in The Netherlands have the same rights as Dutch nationals with regard to pay, working conditions, access to housing, vocational training and education, social security and trade union membership. EC nationals may use the services of Dutch jobcentres, the *Arbeidsbureau* (AB), free of charge; offices can be found in all major towns throughout the country. To find the address of the nearest office, look in the telephone directory or the Dutch equivalent of the Yellow Pages, *Gouden Gids*.

Private employment agencies are the most useful source of temporary employment. However, temporary work via an agency is available for a maximum of six months. It is important to note that under the conditions of a temporary contract instant termination is always possible for both parties. Private agencies are listed under *Uitzendbureaux* in *Gouden Gids*. Some of the largest employment agencies are *BBB, ASB, Randstad, Unique* and *Manpower*.

The press and word-of-mouth recruitment are very important media for finding a job in The Netherlands. Most Dutch nationals and regional newspapers carry job advertisements, especially on Saturdays. Examples are *De Telegraaf, Het Algemeen Dagblad* and *De Volks Courants*, but there are many others including more specialized newspapers, magazines and journals. The most useful of the national daily newspapers for graduates are the *NRC Handelsblad* and *de Volkskrant*.

The Dutch government is closely involved in employment issues. Legislation and policy cover income agreements, minimum wages, equal opportunities, maximum working hours, rest periods and shiftwork. Collective wage agreements are common for many sectors of industry. Fringe benefits are often more generous than in other EC countries and subsidized canteens, savings plans, private pension plans, company cars and crèche facilities are common benefits for many employees.

The Netherlands differs from many EC countries in that there are many English-speaking companies, and for employment within these a knowledge of other languages may not be absolutely essential. International finance is conducted principally in English. The speculative approach to job hunting is common, and two useful directories for this are *Intermediair Jaarboek* and *Kompass Netherlands*; both may be found in public libraries and careers libraries.

Application forms are not as widely used as in other EC countries, most notably Britain and Ireland. The CV forms the most important part of the recruitment and selection procedure. If possible it should be typewritten in Dutch, unless applying to an English-speaking company which has advertised in English. The CV should be accompanied by a short handwritten letter outlining the type of work applied for and the reasons for writing to that company.

INFORMATION POINTS

Education and training

Alida de Jong School
Mariaplaats 4a
35II LH Utrecht

Anke Weidema School
Vondellan Ic
9042 NA Assen

Anna Polak School
H Gerhardstraat 2
1502 CK Zaandam

Annie van Dieren School
Wilhelminapark 55
5041 ED Tilburg

CIBB
(Centrum Innovatie
Beroepsonderwijs Bedrijfsleven)
Verwersstraat 13–15
Postbus 1585
5200 BP's Hertogenbusch

Janneke Dierx School
Oude Vlissingseweg 32a
4336 AD Middelburg

Landelijke Stichting
Vrouwenvakscholen
(National Association for Vocational
Training for Women) and Landelijke
vereniging Paraktijkopleiders
(National Association of Practical
Trainers)
Jan Oomenstraat 39
4854 BB Bavel

Lena de Graf School
Kon Emmakade 119
2518 JJ Den Haag

Ministerie van Onderwijs en
Wetenschappen (Ministry of
Education and Science)
Centrale Directie Voorlichting
Postbus 25000
2700 LZ Zoetermeer

Nederlandse Vereniging van
Opleidingsfunctionarissen
(Netherlands Association of
Training Officers)
Dalenk 7a
7371 De Loenen (GLD)

Vrouwenvakschool Informatica
Amsterdam
Wodenstraat 1–3
1076 CC Amsterdam

Employment

Central Bureau of Statistics
Prinses Beatrixlaan 428
2273 XZ Voorburg

Central Planning Bureau
Van Stolkweg 14
2585 JR The Hague

Equal Opportunities Commission
Muzenstraat 30
2511 VW The Hague

Equal Opportunity Policy
Coordination Department
Ministry for Social Affairs and
Employment
Mauritskade 37
2514 HE The Hague

Equal Opportunities Council
(Emancipatieraad)
Lutherse Burgwal 10
2512 CB The Hague

Forum for Women's Economic
Independence
Janskerkhof 1
3512 BK Utrecht

Social and Cultural Planning Bureau
PO Box 37
2280 AA Rijswijk

Central Bureau voor de
Arbeidsvoorziening (Dutch
Employment Service)
Visseringlaan 26
Postbus 5814
2280 HV Rijswijk (2-H)

Central Office of the Employment
Service
Bureau IABS (International
Placement and Trainee Schemes)
PO Box 437
2280 AK Rijswijk

Ministerie van Sociale Zaken en
Werkgelegenheid
(The Ministry of Social Affairs and
Employment)
Anne von Hannoverstraat 4
2595 BJ The Hague

Netherlands-British Chamber of
Commerce
Holland Trade House
Bezuidenh 181
2594 AH The Hague

Project Bureau 'Bolwerk' (for
information on seasonal and casual
work)
Dorpen 22
1741 EE Schagen

Rijksbelastingen (The Tax Authority)
Stationplein 75
2515 BX The Hague

European Information Centres

The Hague
EVD, Economic Information and
Export Promotion
Euro Info Centre
Bezuidenhoutseweg 151
2594 The Hague

Euro Info Centre Zuid-Holland
Koningskade 30
596 AA The Hague

Diemen-Zuid
EG Adviescentrum voor
Ondernemingen
CIMK-RIMK Instit voor het Midden
en Kleinbedrijf
Euro Info Centre
9 Dalsteindreef
Postbus 112
1100 AC Diemen-Zuid

Enschede
Overijselse Ontwikkelings
Maatschappij NV
Euro Info Centre Oost Nederland
Institutenweg 4
Postbus 545
7500 Am Enschede

Groningen
Noordelijke
Ontwikkelingsmaatschappij
Euro Info Centre
Damsport 1
Postbus 424
9700 Groningen

Helmond
EG-Adviescentrum
NV Induma/BOM
Prins Hendriklaan 21a
Postbus 211
5700 AE Helmond

Nijmegen
EG-Informative Centrum Gelderland
Postbus 38326
6503 Ah Nijmegen

Utrecht
Kamar van Koophandel en
Fabrieken voor Utrecht en
Omstreken
Euro Info Centre
Waterstraat 47
Postbus 48
3500 AA Utrecht

Chapter 11

Portugal

KEY FACTS	
Surface area	92,000 sq km, 35,521 sq miles
Capital	Lisbon
Major towns	Coimbra; ports Porto, Tagus, Guadiana, Setúbal
Form of government	democratic republic
Population	(1990 est)10,528,000, annual growth rate 0.7 per cent
Language	Portuguese
Currency	Escudo
Exports	port wine, sherry, olive oil, resin, cork, sardines, textiles, pottery, pulpwood
Vocational educational institutions	Vocational Training Centres (IEFP); Participated Managment Vocational Training Centres
Awarding Organizations	Institute of Employment and Vocational Training; Ministry of Employment and Social Security; Ministry of Education
Grants	some grants and scholarships available

Vocational qualifications	Vocational Training Diplomas; Vocational Proficiency Certificates; Diplomas
Trends/developments	high unemployment has led to much greater collaboration between employing firms and educational institutions with the aim of solving the problems of finding work for people with skills

EDUCATION SYSTEM

A general law, approved in 1986 and known as *Lei de Bases do Sistema Educativo* – LSBE (law on the bases of the Education System), organizes the system of education in Portugal. The law is administered by the Ministry of Education.

Compulsory education

Compulsory education lasts for nine years, from age 6 to 15. In practice most pupils attend some form of voluntary pre- and post-compulsory schooling. There is only limited availability of state pre-primary education though there are many private kindergartens in the cities. The Ministry of Education is responsible for defining educational standards in kindergartens, but funding mostly comes from the Ministry of Social Security. Primary or basic education is divided into three phases:

1: from age 6 to 10;
2: from age 10 to 12;
3: from age 12 to 15 (usually referred to as lower level secondary education).

Because of a shortage of school buildings, many primary schools operate a shift system; the first shift attends from 8.15 to 13.00, the second from 13.00 to 18.00. A 'normal' school day, operated by just over 50 per cent of classes, is from 9.15 to 16.00, with a two-hour lunch break.

Secondary education is only compulsory until the age of 15. At 15, children have two options if they want to continue their education: grammar schools or technical training. Both routes, referred to as the 10th, 11th and 12th years, take three years, usually from ages 15 to 18. At the end of the 12th year at grammar schools, successful students are presented with the *certificado de fin de estudos secundários*. Technical training lasts for three years and leads to the *diploma de 12 ano de escolaridade*. In some cases students can leave at the end of the 11th year with a vocational qualification.

Special education

Education for children with special learning needs is compulsory from age 6 to 15. In Portugal the system of special classes in mainstream schools is the most common method of integration used. After 15, a student may continue his or her education on a voluntary basis up to his or her 18th birthday.

Administration

In accordance with the Autonomy Law passed in 1988, several Portuguese schools are administratively, academically and financially autonomous and financed by credits from the state. Educational establishments, whether they are publicly, privately or cooperatively owned, must be officially recognized by the state. The Ministry of Education concentrates on budgeting, and delegates many executive and planning duties to regional educational committees.

Finance

State education is funded by the Ministry of Education. State schools are free, though parents are charged for books and stationery. Students in further and higher education can qualify for a loan, plus a standard grant, dependent upon academic results, personal finances and dependants.

VOCATIONAL EDUCATION SYSTEM

Vocational training in Portugal can be undertaken by following one of two routes:

a) by attending a vocational training centre (IEFP). Following this route involves a combination of theoretical and practical learning. A number of centres participate: vocational training centres, secondary schools, management vocational training centres, commercial enterprises. The course, on successful completion, leads to one of the following qualifications:

- a vocational training diploma;
- a vocational training certificate;
- a vocational proficiency certificate.

Government ministers are chiefly responsible for administering this type of training and for awarding qualifications.

b) through following the vocational stream in the 12th year of secondary school, called the *12 ano via profissionalizante*. The 12th year vocational stream prepares specifically for a first level of vocational qualification, by means of instruction and practical exercises in a variety of technological areas. Candidates with this qualification may apply for entry to corresponding courses at higher education level. The vocational stream is organized in several courses with curricula designed to meet the present and future needs of social and economic development in the regions. It is offered in state, private or cooperative secondary education institutions, and also by institutions run by other Ministries, firms or private bodies.

Recognition of vocational qualifications by certificates

In July 1992, within the context of the Agreement on Vocational Training Policy signed by the government and the social partners, a legal system was set up whereby vocational qualifications, acquired as a result of completing training courses undertaken at work, are recognized by means of certificates (Decree-Law 95/92 of 23 May 1992). This system will:

- ensure there is coordination between the recognition of training which is undertaken in employment and of training undertaken in the educational system;
- take into account not only training but also other criteria for practising a profession, in particular those subject to regulation;
- ensure that work experience is acknowledged via objective and justified assessment procedures;
- enable any worker who so wishes to officially register his or her training history which can then be approved by means of a certificate;
- contribute to ensuring that training received in Portugal is recognized in other Member States of the EC and to promoting the equivalence of qualifications.

Two types of certificate will be issued: a vocational training certificate which proves that the holder has met the objectives defined in the teaching programmes or training activities; and a certificate of professional skill which testifies to the holder's ability to perform a certain professional activity as a result of having completed training or having gained work experience.

The training bodies themselves issue the training certificates. Responsibility for the certificates of professional skill is shared by the Institute for Employment and Vocational Training (IEFP) through the agency of public or semi-private vocational training centres and other training bodies, and by the departments and bodies of the various Ministries and of the competent Autonomous Regions.

The system whereby vocational training which is undertaken in employment is recognized via certificates is coordinated by a Permanent Committee which operates in parallel to the Board of Management of the IEFP. The Committee is made up of 16 representatives, eight from Public Administration, four from trade unions and four from employers' confederations. The intention is to set up specialized technical committees which would also be based on tripartite representation and which would come under the responsibility of the Permanent Committee. The aim of these committees will be to define the standards for recognition of training in certain professional sectors. Technical support for the coordination structure is provided jointly by the Directorate General of Employment, and Vocational Training and the departments of the IEFP.

Training grants

In the wake of the Agreement on Vocational Training Policy, and against a background of an upsurge in continuous training, a legal system was set up in 1992 whereby grants for training undertaken on the initiative of the worker are awarded by the IEFP Institute for Employment and Professional Training. IEFP is an organization set up by the Ministry of Employment and Social Security under an Executive Commission, as well as representative bodies from employer and employee organizations. It is a course provider as well as an examining/assessment body and is also responsible for policy development.

Employed or unemployed persons may benefit from the training grants by submitting applications to the Jobcentre. With regard to the award of grants, priorities are:

- workers in sectors or regions experiencing grave difficulties or undergoing restructuring;
- workers in firms experiencing grave difficulties or undergoing restructuring;
- other workers, especially those with a low standard of training.

In order to be able to participate in training activities, employees need to have the agreement of the employer concerned. Contact with the firm is maintained and the basic wage continues to be paid. The firms receive compensation from the IEFP for the basic wage paid and for other costs incurred. The activities are monitored by a tripartite committee appointed by the Board of Management of the IEFP.

Higher education

The Portuguese system of higher education contains both public institutions owned by the state, and private and cooperative institutions. Consequently, there are both public and private universities and higher education institutions.

Entry to a course of higher education is dependent on the subjects studied in the supplementary secondary education course (10th/11th years) and on the subjects studied in the 12th year. Acceptable qualifications for entry into higher education include:

- *12 ano via de ensino* (12th year academic stream);
- *12 ano via profissionalizante* (12th year vocational stream);
- *12 ano via técnico-profissional* (12th year technical vocational stream).

Admissions to universities or other higher education institutes is regulated by one and the same procedure, the so called *concurso nacional* (national admissions procedure). All candidates must fulfil the following requirements:

- presentation of the *certificado de fin de estudos secundários* obtained after successful completion of 12th year schooling (either from having followed the academic stream or the vocational stream);
- submission to the *prova geral de acesso* (entrance examination); this examination does not eliminate candidates, it is merely employed to help list candidates for admission purposes.

Adult education

The agreement on vocational policy signed in 1991 has some direct implications for adult vocational education and training. One of its major aims is stepping up continuing training for the adult workforce. The general intention is twofold: first, that more adults should receive up-dated skills training on a regular basis and, second, that a greater number of enterprises should be encouraged to provide training for their workforces.

Candidates who do not have the 12th year school certificate and are over 25 years of age may apply for entry to a given course in a higher education institution if they pass the special qualifying examination (*exame extraordinario de avalicao de capacidade para acesso ao ensino superior*).

ECONOMIC FEATURES

Portugal has changed dramatically since the 1974 revolution and, in particular, since joining the EC in 1986. In 1989 the Portuguese Constitution was amended to allow all state undertakings to be denationalized.

The new Portugal is one of rising investment and domestic demand, with unemployment down to 5 per cent. Investment has been growing since 1986 following the 1983–85 stabilization programme; investment is led by the British, Spanish and French, mostly in the property, tourism, construction and banking fields but also in agribusiness and food processing.

Employment promotion measures

Financial assistance is available for the creation of jobs and new enterprises. This aid is for the creation of jobs and new enterprises for the purpose of taking on unemployed workers. It is also intended to help young people in finding employment, assist LTUs in setting up their own businesses and to create local employment initiatives.

In the field of vocational training, there is also a planned increase in the training grants for initiatives that are co-financed by the ESF; those workers affected have priority in nominations for operational programmes and employment training programmes.

Beyond the activities of the Ministry of Industry and Energy, there are initiatives which are within the competence of the Ministry of Employment and Social Security, notably a permanent and interdisciplinary steering committee. This will serve as a follow-up in the field of social working conditions, in liaison with the Executive Commission of the OID. Regional information bureaux are being set up in the field of information, advice and vocational orientation to assist people to gain access to vocational training and employment programmes.

Investment incentives

Investment incentives are generous and include the Regional Base Incentive Scheme which allows for up to 65 per cent of total investment depending on location and sectoral interest. Other schemes cover tourism and R&D projects. Total foreign investment in 1989 amounted to some $2.5 billion, five times the level recorded in 1987, with the UK representing 25 per cent of total direct investment. The latest projects include those of Ford Motor Co, General Motors and the Nestlé group.

Of special interest is the Madeira Development Company (SDM) which is located within easy reach of the Atlantic shipping routes, offering manufacturers and assemblers an advantageous stepping stone into Europe, Africa, South and North America. The SDM offers favourable tax arrangements and full EC membership. Altogether, over 150 operating licences have been granted in Madeira, mainly in international services but also in the offshore financial centres, in the industrial zones and in the shipping industry.

Within the framework of the Integrated Operation of Development (*Operação Integrada de Desenvolvimeto* – OID), a new system has been developed in order to accelerate the process of restructuring and industrial modernization of the Ave Valley region. The System of Incentives for Industrial Diversification of the Ave Valley (*Sistema de Incentivos a Diversifiçãcao Industrial do Vale do Ave* – SINDAVE) was created in 1991. It aims to support industrial (non-textile) activities in the region.

The activities aim to create conditions which by progressively reducing the region's excessive dependence on one, single economic activity will enable a variety of alternative activities to be undertaken.

FINDING EMPLOYMENT

EC nationals have the right to live and work in Portugal without a work permit. A full EC passport is essential; a visitor's passport or excursion document is not sufficient. EC nationals are free to enter Portugal for up to three months to look for work or to set up in business. Visitors who intend to stay for longer than three months must apply for a residence permit (*autorização de residência*). Applications should be made to the nearest Ministry of Internal Affairs (*Serviço de Estrangeiros*). An identity card (*bilhete de identidad*) must be carried at all times; application forms for the *bilhete de identidad* are available from any other EC state consulate office in Portugal. Completed forms have to be submitted to the local parish council (*junta de freguesia*).

EC nationals working in Portugal have the same rights as Portuguese nationals with regard to pay, working conditions, access to housing, vocational education and training, social security and trade union membership. They have free access to the Portuguese Employment Service and job centres, *Centro do Emprego*. These are government offices and are administered by the *Ministério de Emprego e Segurança Social*. Their addresses can be found in a telephone directory (*Lista Telefónica*) or the Portuguese equivalent of Yellow Pages, *Páginas Amarelas*.

The majority of private employment agencies are based in Lisbon and Oporto. They are listed in *Páginas Amarelas* under *Pessoal Temporário* (Temporary), and *Pessoal Recrutamento e Selecçao* (Personal Recruitment and Selection). Larger public reference libraries in other EC countries often hold copies of *Páginas Amarelas*. It is important to note that employment agencies are not allowed to place foreign nationals lacking a valid residence permit.

Recruitment fairs are growing in popularity as a method of recruitment and selection. The first was organized by the engineering faculty at the Technical University of Lisbon in 1990. Many more are being planned throughout Portugal in response to the shortages of senior managers, computing staff, accountants and electrical engineers.

The major newspapers in Portugal include *Diário de Notícias, Correio da Manha, Público* and *Jornal de Notícias*. Most carry vacancies every day. The *Diário de Notícias* and *Público* carry most job vacancies in the Lisbon area, while *Jornal de Notícias* is better for vacancies in Oporto. The newspaper *Expresso* (Saturday) is the main source of management and professional vacancies. English-language newspapers such as *Anglo-Portuguese News* (APN), *Portugal Post* and *Algarve News* also advertise vacancies. Most advertisements simply ask for a CV and sometimes a photograph, and salaries are often not mentioned.

Even taking into account the fact that Portugal is one of the cheapest places to live in the EC, salaries are still considerably lower than most of the rest of the EC. There is a minimum wage which is fixed by law, and all full-time employees are also entitled to a Christmas bonus of one month's salary, which is known as the thirteenth month. In addition, a fouteenth month is paid at the end of June for most sectors.

The legal minimum working week in Portugal is 44 hours. There is a limit of two hours overtime daily, or 200 hours annually. The legal rate for overtime is 50 per cent extra for the first hour and 75 per cent for subsequent hours or parts of hours. Work on weekly rest days and holidays receives at least 100 per cent extra. Annual leave entitlement is 22 working days. There are also 12 obligatory public holidays. All companies must have works councils and meet them once a month. Unions represent employees and negotiate collective agreements in many sectors.

INFORMATION POINTS

Education and training

Gabinete Releçóes Internacionais
(Ministry of Education)
Avenida 5 Octubro 35–37
1000 Lisbon

Employment

Associaçáo Luso-Britânica do Porto
(Portuguese-British Association)
Rua do Breiner 155/165
4000 Porto

British Consulate
Rua da Estrela 4
1200 Lisbon

British Council
Rua de São Marçal 174
1294 Lisbon

British Embassy
Rua Sao Domingos á Lapa 35–37
1200 Lisbon

Câmara do Comércio Luso-Britânica
(Portuguese-British Chamber of
Commerce)
Rua da Estrela 8
1200 Lisbon

Centro Nacional de Pensãos
(National Pension Centre)
Campo Grande 6
1771 Lisbon

Departmento de Relaçãos
Internacionais e Convençãos da
Segurança Social (International
social security)
Rua da Junqueira 112
1300 Lisbon

Direcção-Geral das Contribuiços e
Impostos (DGCI)
(Central Government Tax Office)
Rua D Duarte 4
1100 Lisbon

Ministerio do Emprego e Segurança
Social (Ministry of Employment and
Social Security)
Praça de Londres
1000 Lisbon

European Information Centres

Angra Do Heroismo
(antenne/satellite PT-510)
Camera do Comercio e Industrie dos
Açores
Rua da Palha 32/34
9700 Angra Do Heroismo

Aviero
Associação Industrial do Distrito de
Aveiro
Euro Info Centre
Av. Dr Lourenco Peixinho, 146–5 A
3800 Aveiro

Coimbra
(antenne/satellite PT-504)
Associação Comercial e Industrial de
Coimbra
Avenida Sa da Bandeira 90–92
3000 Coimbra

Eurogabinete para a Regiao Centro
Rua Bernardim Ribeiro 80
3000 Coimbra

Evora
Istituto de Apoio as Pequenas e
Medias Empresas e ao Investimento
Eurogabinete PME
Rua do Valasco 19 C
7000 Evora

Faro
Commissao de Coordenação da
Regiao do Algavre
Euro Info Centre
Praca da Liberdade 2
8000 Faro

Funchal (Madeira)
Commissao de Comercial e
Industrial do Funchal/CCI da
Madeira
Eurogabinete da Madeira
Avenida Arriaga 41
9000 Funchal Madeira

Lisbon
Associação Industrial Portuguesa
Eurogabinate
Praça das Industrias
1399 Lisbon

Banco de Fomento e Exterior
Eurogabinete
Av. Casal Ribeiro 59
1000 Lisbon

Caixa Geral de Depositos
Eurogabinete
Av. da Republica 31
1000 Lisbon

Ponta Delgada (Açores)
Norma-Açores e Câmara de
Comércio e Indústria
dos Açores
Eurogabinete dos Açores
Rua Antonio Joaquim Nunes Da
Silva 55
9500 Ponta Delgada – Açores

Porto/Matosinhos
Associação Industrial Portuense
Eurogabinete
Leça da Palmeira
4450 Matosinhos

Chapter 12

Spain

KEY FACTS

Surface area	504,750 sq km, 194,885 sq miles
Capital	Madrid
Major towns	Zaragoza, Seville, Murcia, Cordoba; ports Barcelona, Valencia, Cartegena, Málaga, Cadiz, Vigo, Santander, Bilboa
Form of government	constitutional monarchy
Population	(1990 est) 39,623,000, annual growth rate 0.6 per cent
Languages	Spanish (Castilian, official), and regional languages which are recognized within their own boundaries (Basque, Catalan, Galician, Valencian and Majorcan)
Currency	Peseta
Exports	citrus fruits, grapes, pomegranates, vegetables, wine, sherry, olive oil, canned fruit and fish, iron ore, cork, vehicles, leather goods, ceramics
Vocational educational institutions	Colleges of Vocational Education; Polytechnic Colleges of Vocational Education; Job Training Centres; Institutos

Awarding organizations	Ministry of Education and Science (MEC); Ministry of Labour and Social Security (INEM)
Grants	grants are paid to families with low incomes; in practice only a very small proportion of students receive grant support. Employer subsidies and other financial incentives are available to enhance continuing vocational training
Vocational qualifications	Job Training Diploma; Certificate of Second Level Vocational Education
Trends/developments	emphasis on occupation-specific and localized training through the introduction of Provincial Monitoring Committees for practical vocational training to enable the INEM to implement training

EDUCATION SYSTEM

Most 4- and 5-year-olds attend pre-primary education on a voluntary basis. Kindergartens cater for 2- and 3-year-olds, in a similar way to the home, while nursery schools for 4- and 5-year-olds aim to increase children's potential in grouped activity. The 3Rs are not taught, but pupils are involved in language and pre-numeric activities. About one in ten attend kindergarten, and most other children attend either nursery schools or pre-primary schools, with the latter being by far the most popular option. Pre-primary schools are usually attached to primary schools and about two-thirds of places are in schools run by regional governments or the national Ministry of Education and Science (MEC). In addition, pre-school institutions are managed by the Ministry of Labour, the National Institution for Social Assistance, the municipalities and private bodies.

Almost 70 per cent of schools are in the state sector. Private institutions also exist and many are administered by the Roman Catholic church; they are responsible for the education of almost 30 per cent of Spanish children.

Private education in Spain is not as expensive as in other countries as a result of being partially subsidized by the state.

Compulsory education

Education is compulsory for eight years, from 6 to 14, but is gradually being extended to 16. The school year lasts for 36 weeks, the required weekly attendance being 25 hours. Primary education is referred to as EGB – *Education General Basica*. The school day is usually from 9.00 to 17.00, with a three-hour lunch break.

The lower and intermediate cycles of EGB last for five years, in two cycles: lower – two years; intermediate – three years, with one teacher for all subjects. The recommended syllabus concentrates, for two-thirds of the week, on the native language (Castilian), mathematics, and social and natural science. Artistic, physical and religous education are also included. Progress is monitored by continuous assessment from the pupils' own teacher, and remedial work is organized for slower learners. A 7-year-old without basic skills would automatically remain in the lower cycle of education for an extra year.

The upper cycle of EGB continues at the same school for three years, under subject teachers. The basic primary subjects are extended to cover Spanish literature, a foreign language and social science. Pupils completing their basic education successfully are awarded a graduation certificate, based on tests devised by teachers in their own schools (about two-thirds reached this standard in 1990). Those failing to reach this standard receive a school leaving certificate.

Secondary education

At 14, students can leave full-time education, although in practice most pupils continue to study either academic or vocational studies. Pupils graduating from primary education can enter a three-year academic course to study for the *Bachilerato Unificado Polivalente* (BUP), which lasts for a further three years; successful students are known as *Bachiller*. Alternatively, they may enter the first stage of vocational training, known as *formación professional*. In the first two years of the BUP, the subject range is wide, with certain subjects featuring in one year or the other, eg, history in the first and geography in the second. In the third year, six subject areas are common: foreign languages, geography and history, philosophy, technical/professional activities, religous education and physical education, plus three subjects from one of two groups: either Spanish language and literature, Latin, Greek, mathematics; or Spanish language and literature, natural sciences, physics, chemistry, mathematics. Students must pass in all subjects, but there is no final test. Successful students can proceed to university (after a fourth one-year course), enter the second level of professional training or enter work, but in practice most attempt to enter university.

The *Curso de Orientatión Universitaria* – COU *(University orientation course)*

Students with the BUP or the second level of vocational training (*segundo grado*) who wish to enter university, take a one-year course (many private schools don't provide this course and pupils must transfer to a state school), similar in structure to the third of the BUP, with three common subjects: foreign language, Spanish language and philosophy, and another four from one of two groups; either literature, modern history (both compulsory), and two from Latin, Greek, history of art, mathematics; or mathematics, physics (both compulsory) and two from chemistry, biology, geology, technical drawing. Each university sets selection tests as part of its admissions procedure.

Special education

Special schools are attended by about half of all children with special learning needs, and the rest attend mainstream schools, usually in special education classes. In addition to teachers with specific expertise, a wide variety of other disciplines provide help, eg doctors, psychologists, social workers and various therapists.

Education for children with special educational needs is compulsory for eight years, from 6 to 14.

Administration

Responsibilities for education are distributed between the state and the 17 Autonomous Communities (regional governments). The Constitution lists 32 areas where the state has exclusive responsibility and 22 areas where the Autonomous Communities have administrative powers. The state has exclusive responsibility for the general regulation of the educational system, which includes the length of compulsory schooling, the levels, cycles and teaching methods. It also determines the minimum requirements for educational establishments, comprising the academic qualifications of teachers, teacher:pupil ratios, teaching and sports facilities and the number of school places. The Autonomous Communities manage the education system and cover such areas as teaching staff. The MEC is directly responsible for education. It proposes and implements government policy and is advised by two bodies: the School Council and the National Council for Universities.

A new 'Autonomous Pact' was signed in 1992 by the president of the Spanish government and the leader of the opposition, for the transfer of powers to the Autonomous Communities which did not already have them; they were Madrid, La Rioja, Castilla-La Mancha, Castilla Leon, Baleares, Murcia, Extremadura, Cantabria and Aragon.

Finance

Public expenditure on education accounts for approximately 4 per cent of GNP, the majority of which comes from the MEC. Just over 30 per cent of total education expenditure is derived from the private sector.

The government runs a grant system which is paid to families with low incomes. Slightly more than 10 per cent of university students receive grants, and the same proportion hold scholarships. All grant holders are exempt from paying registration fees. Grants are occasionally linked to school reports, and it may be necessary for students to have passed the last two years of upper secondary school with exceptionally high marks in order to qualify for a grant or other form of financial assistance. Grants may also be awarded for certain expenses only, for example, books or transport.

VOCATIONAL EDUCATION SYSTEM

The Royal Decree (1618/1990) which regulates the National Training and Vocational Integration Plan (plan FIP) was approved by Cabinet on 14 December 1990. This Decree provides the legal basis for Spanish policy on vocational and further training to bring it into the 21st century. It relates to:

- practical vocational training which has a twofold aim: the integration and reintegration of employees into the labour market, and further training in companies;
- cooperation between the labour and education administrations in the fields of adult education and training;
- knowledge of the labour market and qualifications, provided by the Permanent Observatory for Occupational Trends.

The following measures have been introduced by this Royal Decree:

- the establishment of a plan of specific priority actions in the fields of vocational training and guidance and professional integration, which are to benefit the most disadvantaged sectors of the labour market;
- the creation of Provincial Monitoring Committees for Practical Vocational Training (*Committees Provinciales de Seguimiento de la Formacion Profesional Ocupacional*), to enable the general Council of the National Employment Institute (INEM) to implement their institutional participation on a provincial level;
- the implementation of new mechanisms whereby social partners may monitor, receive and exchange information and participate in each other's activities;
- the implementation of training activities into employment policy has

been one of the main objectives of FIP since it was introduced in 1985. Of the measures included in the Royal Decree to increase integration efforts, the following are most significant:

- the promotion of alternated training and the regulation of periods of practical work experience in companies or in suitable training centres for young persons under the age of 25;
- young persons hired on a training contract will be guaranteed training facilities outside the company, and a training course of at least 200 hours, in accordance with labour market demands, if they are unemployed at the end of their contract;
- an increase in vocational guidance;
- the introduction of triennial programme contracts to be signed by employers' organizations and trade unions. These contracts lay down quantitative and financial arrangements and objective-mechanisms for quality control of training, as well as being a means of monitoring implementation of the activities.

The new legal framework has acted as a forerunner to the drafting of the National Vocational Training Programme by the General Council of Vocational Training (CGFP), which has been made possible through the General Regulation of the Education System (LOGSE). From 1992, this programme is designed to link the provision of basic vocational training and specific vocational training, both of which will be managed by the education ministry. It will act as a framework for practical vocational training, managed by the labour administration. Two of the basic functions of the programme as laid down in the Royal Decree are (a) to determine the provision of vocational training managed by the education and labour administrations; and (b) to regulate the uniformity and validity of vocational training, in line with the EC's programme on the equivalence of vocational training qualifications.

Regulated vocational education in Spain is conceived as a form of secondary education following on from compulsory basic education. This stream caters for students who wish to acquire job-related skills, as opposed to traditional general secondary education which basically only leads to higher education. It is also obligatory for students who have only attended, but not actually passed, basic education. Education in Spain is compulsory until 14, although in practice most young people stay on until 16. At 14 a pupil has two options to commence their secondary education:

- the *Bachillerato Unificado y Polivalente* (BUP) – general secondary school – which consists of three years of study (usually from 14 to 17 years of age);
- the *Formación Professional* – vocational education structured in two

stages and known as *primero* or FP1, or *segundo* or FP11 (14–19 years of age).

It should be noted that the Spanish regulations allow for a number of transitions between the academic and vocational streams which enable a student to move from one to the other.

At 16, students proceed to:

- secondary baccalaureat (three years and one as preparation for university);
- vocational schools where they do two years' primary vocational study and then go into employment; or
- vocational schools for three years as preparation for university or employment.

There is no equivalent of a British College of Further Education; the comparable vocational work is done at the top end of the vocational schools. There are many vocational schools in Spain where school and work are combined in a form of dual system, in which students go to work part-time, rather than employees attending school part-time. In such cases, the Ministry of Education pays the firms involved to provide the students with work experience. Although the apprenticeship system is not as well developed in Spain as it is in, say, Denmark and Germany, vocational education has always played a key role in upper secondary education.

Higher education

Students with the BUP on the second level of vocational training who wish to enter university take a one-year university orientation course, *Curso de Orientación Universitario* (COU). There are four options in the COU:

- science and technology;
- social sciences;
- arts and lanuguages;
- biology and medicine.

The COU is a *sine qua non* for entering higher education. In addition, most universities set selection tests for entry.

Universities schools offer a three-year course on various vocational subjects, such as nursing, engineering, computing or teaching for basic general education, leading to a *diplomada*. Those students with a *diplomada* can transfer to the second cycle of universities offering longer courses.

The geographical distribution of students is uneven, with about two-fifths in 1985 qualifying from either Madrid or Barcelona. About half of the students are women. Other establishments provide a five-year course, beginning with a three-year basic course, followed by a two-year specialization, leading to the title *Licenciado*. A further two-year course, including a written thesis, yields a *doctorate*. Nearly half these students are women.

Teacher training

The course of studies for primary school teachers lasts for three years, which start after completion of the BUP and the COU and leads to a diploma.

All secondary school teachers have to receive both their scientific and pedagogical training at universities. Institutes of Education Sciences are responsible for giving a course of theory and practice with a total duration of 300 hours, leading to the Certificate of Pedagogical Aptitude (CAP).

Teaching staff at university level receive instruction in their basic subject at the university itself, and gain teaching practice by being assistant lecturers.

Adult education

The Ministry of Education and Science (MEC) runs a programme of education for adults. A higher proportion of women than men participate in higher education, and there are more students attending public sector centres than private sector centres.

There are opportunities for adults to take part in all standards of education as day release or at night schools, from the EGB, leading to the School Graduate title of the Certificate of Studies, to secondary and university education leading to a degree or diploma. Distance learning, open university and self-development modular learning is very highly developed in Spain and inhabitants of rural communities living a considerable distance from a vocational training centre can still benefit from schemes on offer.

ECONOMIC FEATURES

From Spain's earlier isolation and quite backward economy during the Franco years, the country has emerged with a new democratic constitution which is clearly working. Since being accepted as a full member of the EC in 1986, Spanish business and construction projects have been booming and foreign investment and money continues to pour in – over $30 billion in the period 1989–92. Today, it is a country of powerful incentive packages and liberalized laws on the repatriation of profit and

Spain

capital that have helped to fuel an economic renaissance unparalleled on the European continent. Thousands of miles of new highways are being built to accommodate growing motor freight traffic and the rising tide of new vehicles that prosperity has brought to Spain. New rail, road and telecommunications projects are opening up the 15 autonomous regions (*Communicades Autonomas*) which together with the Balearic and Canary Islands make up the state of Spain and its population of 39.6 million. It is Europe's fifth largest consumer market, and growing.

Employment rates are highest in the largest cities: Madrid, Barcelona, Valencia, Seville, Zaragoza, Málaga, Bilbao and Murcia. As Spain continues to modernize its infrastructure and foster more industry, the nature of its workforce and the sophistication of its population is changing quite rapidly. Much of Spain is still, however, relatively underdeveloped; unemployment has averaged 16 per cent per annum since the late 1980s, and is as high as 50 per cent in areas dominated by declining heavy industry.

However, low labour costs and a ready pool of labour combined with high levels of financial subsidy and EC approved incentives, together with low cost but high quality life style in a Mediterranean climate, contribute to the many advantages afforded to the new investor. Opportunities include:

- the introduction of state-of-the-art technologies and enterprise as business and science parks are developed to north European standards;
- manufacturing opportunities in priority development zones;
- Hispano-American linked projects as Spanish-speaking populations expand in both North and South America;
- a growing market for tourism and leisure-related projects and equipment;
- an increasing demand for high added value food and agribusiness products.

As regards financial incentives for inward investment programmes, new regional incentive schemes were introduced in 1987. These are discretionary and available to eligible manufacturing, service and extractive projects. The grant schemes apply to three kinds of assisted areas agreed by an interministerial board. Under a Royal Decree of December 1987, zones and maximum grants available towards eligible expenditure are defined, grants varying from 20 per cent to as high as 75 per cent in parts of Extremadura in the south-west and Galicia in the extreme north-west (compared with a maximum of 30 per cent under the previous system). Maximum 50 per cent grants are available in Murcia, Andalucia in the south as well as in the Canary Islands and parts of Aragon, Castilla-Leon and Castilla-La Mancha. Lower levels of grants are available in Asturias and Cantabria. These are amongst the highest regional grants available in the EC and there are also corporate tax concessions widely available. The regional incentives are centralized through Spain's Directorate General of Regional Economic Incentives. The system includes three *zonas*, which are similar to US state enterprise zones:

- ZPEs, *Zonas de Promocion Economica*, or Economic Promotion Areas, are geographical zones of the country with low levels of development. Maximum subsidies in these areas range from 30 to 50 per cent of a company's total investment. Most of Spain is classed ZPE.
- ZIDs, *Zonas Industrializadas en Declive* or Industrial Areas in Decline, are zones in the throes of major industrial change. Maximum subsidies in these areas can be as high as 75 per cent of total investment
- ZEs, *Zonas Especiales* or Special Zones, are designated when the government decides they are required by special circumstances; subsidies can go up to 20 per cent.

Many American manufacturers are already benefiting from one or more of these subsidies. The Hughes Aircraft Corporation in the region of Andalucia, for example, is reportedly about 40 per cent subsidized. DuPont's NOMEX textile plant in Asturias received a 35 per cent subsidy for its initial direct investment. The new AT & T facility in Madrid has been followed by Ford Electronics in Cadiz and General Electric in Murcia. The Japanese heavyweights are also moving in to take advantage of the growing economy. Spain is particularly interested in technology industries including telecommunications, pharmaceuticals, electronics, advanced materials, biotechnology, automotive parts and food-processing equipment. Pollution control and waste management technologies are also a good bet, because of the increased emphasis European countries are placing on environmental issues. While Spain offers a growing domestic market with opportunities still to spare, it offers much more as a platform from which to address the EC, a marketplace of 320 million people.

While the governments of each of the Autonomous Communities have established development agencies to promote their regions, implement grant provision and assist investors at all stages of their projects, general information is available from the Directorate General of Regional Economic Incentives of the Ministry of Economy and Finance in Madrid; another useful contact is the *Sociedad Estatal de Promocion y Equipamiento de Suelo* (SEPES), the state development agency, also in Madrid.

Economic measures to improve vocational education

A number of important initiatives have been introduced in Spain since 1990 which affect vocational education and access to training. Since the end of December 1991, the National Institute for the Development of the Social Economy (INFES) has assumed the functions and tasks of the dismantled Directorate General for Cooperatives and Workers Companies. The institute was created by Law 31/1990 of 27 December 1990 on general state expenditure. INFES is an autonomous administrative body falling under the Ministry of Labour and Social Security, as a management body of policy on the social economy. Royal Decree 1836/1991 of 28 December 1991 defines the basic structure and functions of the institute and attributes to it the following tasks:

- coordination with the ministerial departments which implement promotional activities in the economy (cooperatives, consumer associations, workers' organizations);
- signature of agreements and conventions with the Autonomous Communities, local corporations, universities; and the establishment of coordination links and cooperation with international bodies and institutions;
- facilitating a means of financing economic enterprises and associations through the creation, management, follow-up and monitoring of subsidy and assistance programmes, and the participation in financial initiatives for enterprise.

With the Royal Decree 1/1992 of 3 April 1992 on Urgent Measures for Employment Promotion and Protection in case of Unemployment, the government has adopted a number of measures which, on the one hand, enable the allocation of public funds for active employment policies, which aim to stimulate permanent employment for categories of workers who have particular difficulties integrating professionally, and offer better training to the unemployed. On the other hand, the measures enable a rationalization of expenditure for protection in the case of unemployment, so as to ensure the future financial balance of the system and to offer efficient protection for the unemployed who are actively in search of a job.

The Decree establishes the following economic incentives for the employment of certain categories of workers:

- a subsidy of 400,000 pesetas for an employer who hires a person aged under 25 years who has been unemployed for longer than one year, or a person aged between 25 and 29 who has not worked for more than three months beforehand;
- a subsidy of 500,000 pesetas and a 50 per cent reduction of

employers' social security contributions for hiring a worker aged over 45 years who has been out of work for more than a year;

- a subsidy of 500,000 pesetas for recruiting a woman who has been unemployed for more than one year, in professions or occupations where women are under-represented, or for recruiting a woman aged over 25 years who wishes to reintegrate into paid employment after a career break of more than five years;
- a subsidy of 550,000 pesetas for each practical work contact or training contract which is converted into a permanent employment contract. At the same time, the reduction of employers' contributions which applied to the two forms of training contracts will be abolished.

By Royal Decree 3/1992 of 10 January 1992, the government has established the minimum interprofessional wage which has been in force since 1 January 1992, for permanent, non-permanent and domestic workers. The amount of the new minimum wage has increased by over 5 per cent compared to that of 1991. This increase takes account of the estimated rate of inflation for 1992 (5 per cent), the readjustment of the inflation rate for 1991, increased productivity, and the development of labour's share in the national income and the general economic situation. It is part of a policy which aims to increase the vitality of economic activity and the competitiveness of the Spanish economy, and therefore aims to contain inflation and to impose minimum wage moderation. The minimum monthly wages for any activity in the agricultural, industrial or service sectors, for either male or female workers are 56,280 pesetas for workers who are aged 18 or over, and 37,170 pesetas for workers aged under 18. Annual minimum wages have been fixed at 787,920 pesetas or 520,380 pesetas depending on whether the workers are 18 years old or younger.

FINDING EMPLOYMENT

EC nationals have the right to live and work in Spain without a work permit. A full EC passport is required; a visitor's passport or excursion document is not sufficient. EC nationals can enter Spain for up to three months to look for work or set up in business. Visitors who intend to stay for over three months require a residence card (*tarjeta de residencia*). This is issued by local authorities, usually the local police headquarters, and should be applied for within 15 days of arrival. A profession peculiar to Spain is that of a *gestor*. *Gestors* can be approached to carry out all the time-consuming and frustrating work associated with obtaining a residence permit (or any other administrative requirement). *Gestors'* offices (*gestorias*) are listed in *Páginas Ammarillas*. Prices vary considerably between *gestors*, so it is worth shopping around. Anyone entering

Spain to set up their own business in some form of self-employment does not require a work permit, but still has to register with the local police station once in Spain.

EC nationals working in Spain have the same rights as Spanish nationals with regard to pay, working conditions, access to housing, vocational education and training, social security and trade union membership. They also have free access to Spanish job centres, *Oficianos de Empleo* which are run by the *Instituto Nacional de Empleo* (INEM). The state-run INEM is the only employment and recruitment agency allowed to operate in Spain for permanent work; private agencies in Spain are only allowed to operate for temporary job placements. They are listed in telephone directories and *Páginas Amarillas* under *Empresas de Trabajo Temporal.*

Oficianos de Empleo are located in all major cities and towns, their addresses can be found in the telephone directory, *La Guiá Telefonica*, often referred to as just *La Guia*. INEM has no special services for graduates, but in conjunction with 14 Spanish universities has set up *Centros de Orientación e Información de Empleo* (COIEs), which is predominantly a placement service. Some other universities have set up their own independent placement services, usually known as *Bolsas de Trabajo*. These services, however, are generally available only to the students of the institutions providing them.

All major newspapers in Spain carry job advertisements. They include *El País, ABC, El Mundo, Diario 16* and *Ya*. Sunday editions have the largest recruitment sections. All regional newspapers also have vacancy sections; they include *La Vanguardia* (for Catalonia), and *La Gaceta del Norte* (for the Bilbao region). English-language publications such as *Lookout,* which circulates on the Costa del Sol, also advertise vacancies. These are predominantly for the hotel, catering and tourist industries. A student magazine called *Campus* was introduced in 1991 and also advertises vacancies. Some standard reference books which may be useful in identifying employers to target are produced annually or biennially and include *Kompass*, the *Directoria de Sociedades, Consejeros Y Directivos, Las 2,000 Mayores Empresas Espanolas* and *5,000 Espana*.

The main recruitment season is between January and May. Job applications are usually expected to include a handwritten letter, a typed CV (in Spanish) and often photocopies of certificates, diplomas and other relevant qualifications, as well as a recent photograph. In large companies, an initial interview is often followed by psychometric tests and then a series of lengthier interviews, frequently up to five or more. The ability to speak Castilian (referred to by the rest of the EC as Spanish) is essential throughout Spain. Some knowledge of the regional languages is also advantageous, especially in Catalonia (Catalan), Galicia (Galician) and the Basque country (Euskera).

There is a minimum wage which is fixed annually by the Spanish government, and there are also collective agreements for many sectors. A peculiar aspect of the Spanish pay practice is the distribution of two extra payrolls every year, one at Christmas and one in summer. These are known as *pagas extraordinarias*.

The normal working week is 40 hours. Overtime is voluntary and cannot exceed 80 hours per year. By law, it must be paid at a rate not less than 175 per cent of normal hourly rates. The traditional afternoon siesta followed by a late evening closing time is now being replaced by a more modern European one-hour lunch break and earlier finish, particularly in many of the larger international businesses which have permanent establishments in Spain. Annual leave entitlement is 30 working days, and there are also 12 days obligatory national public holiday plus two days' regional public holidays. There are statutory rights to paid leave for marriage (15 days). All businesses with 50 or more employees are required to have some form of workplace representation.

INFORMATION POINTS

Education and training

Instituto de Ciencias de la Educacion (ICE)
Escuela Superior de Ingenieros de Caminos ciudad Universitaria
28040 Madrid

Instituto Nacional de Empleo (INEM)
Condesa de Venadito 9
28027 Madrid

Ministerio de Educacion y Ciencia
C/ Alcala 34
28014 Madrid

Employment

British Chamber of Commerce in Spain
Plaza Santa Barbera 10
28010 Madrid

Consejo Superior da las Cámaras Oficiales de Comercio Industría y Navegacion (Chamber of Commerce)
C/ Claudio Coello 19
28001 Madrid

Direccion General de Tributos (Tax)
C/ Alcalá 5
28014 Madrid

Ministerio de Economia y Hacienda
C/ Alcalá 11
Madrid

European Information Centres

Albacete
Confederacion Regional de
Empresarios de Castilla la Mancha
Centro Europeo de Informacion
Empresarial
C/ del Rosario 29, 4 Planta
02001 Albacete

Alicante
Grupo Banco Popular Español
Euroventanilla
Rambla de Méndez Nunez 12
03002 Alicante

Barcelona
Banco de Credito Industrial –
Corporacion Bancaria de España SA
Euro Info Centre
Manilla 56–58
08034 Barcelona

Camara Oficial de Comercio,
Industria y Navegacion
de Barcelona
Euro Info Centre
Avenida Diagonal, 452–454
08006 Barcelona

CIDEM/FTN Centro Europeo de
Informacion
Empresarial-Eurofinestreta
Av. Diagonal 403 1r
08008 Barcelona

Bilbao
Camera Oficial de Comercio
Industria y
Navegacion de Bilao
Centro Europeo de Informacion
Empresariel
Alameda de Recalde 50
48008 Bilbao

Caceres
Sociedad para el Desarrollo
Industrial de Extremadura (Sodiex)
Euro Info Centre
C/ Dr. Maranon 2
10002 Caceres

Cordovilla – Pamplona
Asociacion de la Industria Navarra
Euro Info Centre
PO Box 439
31191 Cordovilla – Pamplona

Donostia San Sebastian
Euroventanilla del pais Vasco
C/ Thomas Gros, No 3 Bajo
20001 Donostia San Sebastian

Las Palmas De G Canaria
Consejeria de Economia y Hacienda
Euro Info Centre
C/Nicolás Estévanez 33
35007 Las Palmas De G Canaria

Logroño
Federation de Empresarios de la
Rioja
Euro Info Centre
C/ Hermanos Moroy 8–4
26001 Logroño

Madrid
Camera de Comercio e Industria de
Madrid
Euro Info Centre
Plaza de la Independencia 1
28001 Madrid

Confederacion Española de
Organizaciones de Empresariales
Euro Info Centre
Diego de Leon 50
28006 Madrid

IMPI – ICEX
Centro Europeo de Informacion
Empresarial
Euroventanilla
Paseo de la Castellana, 141–2a
Planta
28046 Madrid

Instituto Madrileño de Desarrollo
(IMADE)
Euroventanilla
Mariano Ron 1
28902 Madrid

Málaga
Banesto
Centro Europeo de Informacion
Plaza de la Constitucion 9
29008 Málaga

Murcia
Instituto de Fomento de la Region de
Murcia
Euro Info Centre
Plaza San Agustin 5
30005 Murcia

Oviedo (Asturias)
(antenne/satellite ES-218)
Federacion Asturiana de Empresarios
C/ Doctor Alfredo Martinez 6-2 pl
33005 Oviedo (Asturias)

Oviedo/Llanera
Instituto de Fomento Regional
del Principado de Asturias
Euro Info Centre
Parque Technologico de Asturias
33420 Llanera

Palma de Mallorca
Consorcio Centro de Documentacion
Europa Islas Baleares
C/ Patronato Obero 30
07006 Palma de Mallorca

Santiago de Compostela
Confederacion de Empresarios de
Galicia
Euro Info Centre
C/ Romero Donallo 7A – Entesuelo
15706 Santiago de Compostela

Seville
Confederacion de Empresarios de
Andalucia
Centro Europeo de Informacion
Empresarial de Andalucia
Avda San Francisco Javier 9
Edificio Sevilla 2–9a Planta
41018 Seville

Toledo
Camera de Comercio e Industria de
Toledo
Euro Info Centre
Plaza San Vincente 3
45001 Toledo

Valencia
Camera Oficial de Comercio,
Industria y Navegacion de Valencia
Euro Info Centre
C/ Poeta Querol, 15
46002 Valencia – Espana

Valladolid
Sodical
Euro Info Centre
C/ Claudio Moyano, 4–1
47001 Valladolid

Zaragoza
Confederacion Regional de
Empresarios de Aragon
Euro Info Centre
Plaza Roma, F-1, 1a Planta
50010 Zaragoza

Chapter 13

United Kingdom

KEY FACTS

Surface area	244,100 sq km, 94,247 sq miles
Capital	London
Major towns	Birmingham, Glasgow, Leeds, Sheffield, Liverpool, Manchester, Edinburgh, Bradford, Bristol, Belfast, Newcastle upon Tyne, Cardiff
Form of government	liberal democracy
Population	(1990 est) 57,121,000, annual growth rate 0.1 per cent
Languages	English, Welsh, Gaelic
Currency	Pound sterling
Exports	cereals, rape, sugar beet, potatoes, meat and meat products, poultry, dairy products, electronic and telecommunications equipment, engineering equipment and scientific instruments, oil and gas, petrochemicals, film and television programmes
Vocational educational institutions	Colleges of Further Education; private sector training providers
Awarding organizations	RSA, BTEC, SCOTVEC, City & Guilds of London Institute

Grants	grants available for post-compulsory education; some scholarships available for specialized training and for certain educational institutions; employer sponsorship programmes also available to enable students to combine paid work with study
Vocational qualifications	NVQs, SVQs, GNVQs, BTEC and SCOTVEC certificates and diplomas
Trends/developments	a range of training measures have been introduced by the Training and Enterprise Councils (TECs) to improve the employment/training interface. The emphasis is on on-going training being available throughout an employee's working life

EDUCATION SYSTEM

The state education system in the UK comprises some state nursery schools (up to the age of 5), primary schools (age 5–7), junior schools (ages 7–11) middle schools and secondary schools (ages 11–16). Sixteen is the minimum leaving age.

Compulsory education

Compulsory primary schooling begins at 5, but many 4-year-olds attend primary school on a voluntary basis. Primary schooling is generally from 9.00 to 15.30, with one hour for lunch. At the end of six years' primary schooling most pupils in the state sector transfer to a comprehensive secondary school. In some areas, grammar schools operate and parents may opt to send their children there. City Technology Colleges (CTCs) offer a third option in secondary education, but these are only available in a very few areas.

Secondary schools in England, Wales and Northern Ireland offer courses leading to the General Certificate of Secondary Education (GCSE), and in Scotland courses are offered leading to the Scottish Certificate of Education (SCE). Children study the National Curriculum and in the third year of the secondary school begin courses leading to GCSE examinations. Each pupil keeps a National Record of Achievement (NRA), in which they may keep a list of achievements, both academic and practical, to present to future employers. From here the options in further education include sixth form colleges, colleges of further education, and Youth Training (YT). Also, courses leading to the International Baccalaureate (IB) are offered at an increasing number of British schools. The diploma is awarded at the end of a two-year period of study, paralleling the A-level years, to those students who have met its wide ranging requirements in six study fields, and been awarded a total score of 24 or more.

Admission to higher education requires a further two years of study from 16 to 18. Acceptable qualifications include A-levels, BTEC national diplomas, or four or five passes at the Scottish Higher Grade level (highers) in the SCE. All are obtained after the GCSE or SCE. In general, two or three A-levels are taken, as compared to seven or eight GCSEs.

Altogether there are about 600 institutions in Great Britain and Northern Ireland which offer higher education courses; all receive their principal funding from one of two sources: central government via the Department for Education (DfE), and the local education authorities.

The National Curriculum

The National Curriculum has been designed to enable children to achieve higher standards by setting demanding national targets for pupils of all ages and abilities. It consists of ten subjects; at the centre are the core subjects of English, mathematics and science. The other subjects are technology, history, geography, a modern foreign language, art, music and physical education. In Wales, Welsh is also part of the National Curriculum. It will be fully in place by the mid-1990s.

Special education

The organization and management of special education provision in the UK falls within the remit of the local education authorities. LEAs must provide education for all children with special learning needs between the ages of 5 and 16. In addition, the Further and Higher Education Act 1992 has removed further education colleges and sixth-form colleges from local education authority control and has set up funding councils. The councils must find suitable courses for students up to the age of 25 with learning difficulties. They also have to provide independent living and communication skills courses which lead to a vocational or academic course.

Administration

Education is controlled centrally by the Department for Education (DfE), and locally through local education authorities (LEAs). The education system is monitored locally through Her Majesty's Inspectorate (HMI). The Education (Schools) Act 1992 has introduced a league table to compare schools' examination performance and increased the power of HMI.

Finance

State education is free. Means-tested grants and interest-free loans are available for students in higher education. As well as the state education system, there are a large number of private and fee-paying schools in the UK which can cater for pupils from 3 years old upwards.

VOCATIONAL EDUCATION SYSTEM

The chief providers of vocational education in the UK are maintained colleges. This stems from the arrangements to which the 1944 Education Act gave expression, placing upon each LEA responsibility to ensure the adequate availability of further education in its area. Colleges have always received income from more than one source, notably from fees from students and employers alongside general recurrent funding from the maintaining LEA. Pressure to cultivate multiple sources of funding has grown in recent years, partly from the squeeze on local authority financing, partly from the growth of government programmes and partly from the recently enhanced freedom afforded to colleges to targeting earned income and using it at their discretion. This freedom, and others concerning the deployment of their budget, flowed particularly from the provisions of the 1988 Education Act, which accorded much increased powers to college governors at the expense of the authority of the LEA. The Further and Higher Education Act 1992 has removed further education colleges and sixth form colleges from local authority ownership, in order to give them independence and enable them to flourish in a market environment.

The origins of Examining and Validating Bodies (EVBs) lie in the aspirations for national, or in some cases, regionally recognized vocational qualifications. This sentiment is increasingly being endorsed by educational institutions as well as employing organizations, as in general, portability of qualifications is seen as important to the effective working of the labour market.

The chief EVBs today, each occupying to some extent its own territory although not so confined by its constitution or by government are:

- The Business & Technology Education Council (BTEC);
- City & Guilds of London Institute (CGLI);
- The Royal Society of Arts Examination Board (RSA).

Many others, however, also have a place stretching across more than one occupation or area, and there are, besides, many professional bodies examining at the relevant level.

Since the mid-1980s there has been a revolution in vocational training and education in the UK. The advent of new vocational qualifications has involved a fundamental rethink of the way we train and educate people for employment. The status of vocational education and training has been awarded a much higher profile through the introduction of National Vocational Qualifications (NVQs), Scottish Vocational Qualifications (SVQs) and General National Vocational Qualifications (GNVQs), which receive accreditation through the National Council of Vocational Qualifications (NCVQ) and the Scottish Council for Vocational Qualifications (SCOTVEC). The NCVQ was set up by the government in 1986 to promote, develop, implement and monitor a comprehensive system of vocational qualifications in England, Wales and Northern Ireland.

NVQs are based on accepted standards of competence and performance established by some 170 Industrial Lead Bodies (ILBs) under the sponsorship of the Training Agency (TA). Each NVQ/SVQ is made up of a number of units or modules and credits can be awarded for each unit. An individual can accumulate NVQ/SVQ unit credits within their own time-scale; there are no time limits for achieving a qualification, so qualifications can be obtained over a period of years in a way which suits candidates and their employers. A key element of the system is the National Record of Vocational Achievement (NROVA). The use of NROVA is made possible when qualifications are offered in the form of a number of component units which can be separately assessed and certificated, as required for NVQs.

In 1992, general SVQs were introduced, similar in most major respects to the GNVQ. General vocational qualifications have been designed to meet the needs of young people in colleges and training centres, and those wanting to return to work, for accessible yet flexible vocational qualifications. They offer students the chance to prepare for work, training, or further study, without prejudicing their future choices. A primary objective for these qualifications is to provide an alternative route leading to employment or higher education for the increasing number of 16-year-olds staying in full-time education. This trend is not only due to the scarcity of jobs for 16-year-olds but also to the higher levels of education that are common in the developed world, with the majority of young people in the EC, North America and Japan staying on in full-time education until 18. GNVQ level 3 will provide a genuine alternative to A-level. From September 1993, students can study GNVQs at two levels: level 2, which equates to a BTEC First or 4 GCSEs. or level 3, which equates to a BTEC National or A-levels.

The subjects which can be studied to GNVQ level are:

- art and design;
- business;
- health and social care;
- leisure and tourism;
- manufacturing.

GNVQ courses have been designed to evolve; they will change as new information and more modern techniques become available. Similarly, more subjects at GNVQ level will be made available as more courses are designed.

The following definitions provide a guide to the levels at which NVQs may be accredited:

- *Level 1*: competence in the performance of work activities which are in the main routine and predictable, or provide a broad foundation, primarily as a basis for progression.
- *Level 2*: competence in a broader and more demanding range of work activities involving greater individual responsibility and autonomy than at level 1.
- *Level 3*: competence in skilled areas that involve performance of a broad range of work activities, including many that are complex and non-routine. In some areas, supervisory competence may be a requirement at this level.
- *Level 4*: competence in the performance of complex, technical, specialized and professional work activities, including those involving design, planning and problem-solving, with a significant degree of personal accountability. In many areas competence in supervision or management will be a requirement at this level.
- *Level 5*: competence in all professional areas above that of level 4. It includes the ability to apply a significant range of fundamental principles and techniques, which enable an individual to assume personal responsibility in design, analysis and diagnosis, planning and problem-solving. Extensive knowledge and understanding are required to underpin competence at this level.

Appreciating the fact that vocational qualifications do not translate into academic qualifications, a useful broad comparison can nevertheless be made:

> *Level 2*: five GCSE or SCE passes at grade C;
> *Level 3*: two A-level passes;
> *Level 4*: Higher National Diploma or Certificate;
> *Level 5*: degree.

The main characteristics of NVQs/SVQs are that they are:

- employer-led (NVQs and SVQs attest to a candidate's competence in a particular occupational area, as measured against standards drawn up by the industry itself);
- competence-based (competence is defined as the ability to perform the activities within an occupation, and embodies the ability to transfer skills and knowledge to new situations within the occupational area);
- criterion-referenced;
- not time-based;
- independent of method;
- available without restriction.

The major benefits of NVQs and SVQs are:

- they give a simple system of vocational qualifications which will encourage employers to train staff, motivate individuals to learn, and help to keep the UK economy competitive;
- NVQs are a nationwide system of vocational qualifications;
- NVQs are directly relevant to employment;
- through NVQs and SVQs, qualifications are much more clearly related to employment standards and needs than previously, and there are clear routes for career or qualifications progression;
- the barriers on training have been removed, and the NVQ/SVQ approach to training is much more flexible. Because they are based on building up credits, there is no requirement to gain qualifications within a specified period, or at a particular place of training, or within restricted age limits.

NVQs/SVQs are a main feature of national training programmes in the Training and Enterprise Councils (TECs) and, north of the border, in the Local Enterprise Companies (LECs). In fact, at the heart of each of these educational changes the melting pot of the TEC network connects the whole vocational education system. TECs are able to help individuals, educational institutions and employing organizations to master the business/education interface. Promoting and managing economic and educational change has rapidly become an essential feature of the TEC movement.

Many trainees commence study towards acquiring NVQs during a two-year period spent on Youth Training (YT). YT has four key objectives:

- achievement of qualifications equivalent to NVQ level 2 as the minimum attainment for young people on the programme;
- a strong emphasis on still higher level skills, particularly at craft and technician level;
- improved job-finding for young people;

- appropriate quality provision for young people with special needs.

Higher education

Altogether about 600 institutions in Great Britain and Northern Ireland offer higher education courses. With the exception of the University of Buckingham, all receive their principal funding from one of two sources: central government via the DfE, and LEAs. HMI plays a major role in the setting up and maintaining of standards in higher education.

The general requirement for admissions to higher education, whether universities or institutes or colleges of higher education is the possession of:

- the General Certificate of Secondary Education (GCSE) A-level (at least 2 passes), or Scottish Highers;
- the BTEC National Diploma or Certificate;
- the International Baccalaureate; or
- the European Baccalaureate.

Universities award either diplomas or degrees, usually after three years of full-time study. An increasing number of organizations, however, are providing part-time degrees over a five- or six-year period. Undergraduate degree courses lead to the award of a Bachelor's degree, with or without honours. Post-graduate degrees, called Master's degrees, follow successful completion of a good first degree.

Adult education

Adults who wish to continue their education are well catered for in the UK. A number of options exist including:

- local colleges of further education which run day courses (sometimes called access courses) for unemployed adults and night school courses in a range of subjects, both academic and vocational;
- private training organizations which often run free or subsidized training courses for adults, particularly for women returners;
- a number of specific courses for older people are provided by organizations such as the University of the Third Age (U3A), Age Concern and the Pre-Retirement Association(PRA);
- the Open University ;
- distance learning and correspondence courses;
- many Training and Entreprise Councils (TECs) run courses in their local areas for continuing vocational training.

Other initiatives in the field of vocational training

Training credits

The term 'training credit' has been applied to a scheme under which young people who leave full-time education before they are 18 are eligible for notional cash sums from public sources to be spent on their training towards acquisition of a NVQ level 2 or higher. By notional cash sums is meant that the credit has a cash-equivalence; it is not convertible into cash, only into training provided.

It has been piloted in a few areas since mid-1990, and training credits are to be made available nationwide by 1996. Universality, however, does not betoken uniformity. TECs are, and will continue to be, the operators of the training credit scheme, and each has some freedom to settle both the substantive features of its scheme and how it will function. Underlying the introduction of training credits are two main beliefs. First, that possession of a training credit will change attitudes among young people, motivating them to insist on training as a component of the jobs they may take. Second, that their operation will promote a consumer-led market and so exert influence on providers to become more effective and efficient.

Another initiative along similar lines which more than one TEC has put in place is the 'smart card' device, whereby increments of training are debited from the card and corresponding payments are made to the training providers.

Investors in People initiative

The Investors in People initiative was launched by the Secretary of State for Employment in November 1990. It is designed to help organizations make a permanent commitment to staff training and development, by setting a rigorous national standard, based on best practice drawn from a wide range of businesses. Companies are encouraged to take a strategic approach to training and development, by linking it to their business objectives.

The initiative has been piloted in England and Wales by TECs, and in Scotland by LECs, working with local organizations. Acheievement of the standard requires that an organization:

- makes a public commitment from the top, to develop all employees to achieve its business objectives;
- regularly reviews the training and development needs of all employees;
- trains and develops individuals on recruitment, and throughout their employment;

- evaluates the investment in training and development, to assess achievements and make improvements for the future.

All employees should have a clear vision of where their organization is going and what personal contribution they can make to its success. When an organization feels that all these requirements have been met, it can apply to the TEC/LEC for assessment as to whether it meets the standard. Evidence must be presented for each area, which is reviewed by a professional assessor. The final decision as to whether the organization can be recognized as an Investor in People is taken by the TEC/LEC Board. This status is reviewed at least every three years.

At the end of the first year of the initiative, 28 British companies had acheived the standard and were awarded Investor in People status. A further 600 organizations, in both the public and private sectors (including the Employment Department Group) had announced their commitment to achieving the standard.

National education and training targets

National education and training targets were published in 1991 by the Confederation of British Industry (CBI). Their general aim is to improve the skill level of the British workforce and the overall efficiency of British industry. The targets focus on the whole population, both young people (foundation learning) and the adult workforce (lifetime learning). They are:

Foundation learning:
- by 1997, 80 per cent of young people to reach NVQ/SVQ 2 (or equivalent of four GCSE passes at grades A–C or four SCE passes 1–3);
- training and education to NVQ/SVQ 3 (or equivalent of two A-level passes or three Scottish highers) available to all young people who can benefit;
- by the year 2000, 50 per cent of young people to reach NVQ/SVQ level 3 (or equivalent);
- education and training provision to develop self reliance, flexibility and breadth.

Lifetime learning:
- by 1996, all employees should take part in training or development activities;
- by 1996, 50 per cent of the workforce to aim for NVQ/SVQs or units towards them;
- by 2000, 50 per cent of the workforce qualified to at least NVQ/SVQ level 3 (or equivalent);

- by 1996, 50 per cent of medium to large organizations to be 'Investors in People'.

National baselines have been set from which to work. TECs and LECs are leading in setting local baselines and targets for both foundation and lifetime learning. The rationale underlying the introduction of national education and training targets is that Britain needs to have a highly skilled and competitive workforce to bring it economic success in the 21st century.

ECONOMIC FEATURES

The UK has a population of 57.1 million and a labour force of 28 million divided between England, Scotland, Wales and Northern Ireland. England is the largest country in the UK with a population of over 47 million. Wales is on England's western border and has a population of 3.2 million and a labour force of 1.2 million. Scotland is located north of England, bordered on the west by the Atlantic Ocean and on the east by the North Sea. It has a population of 5.1 million and a labour force of 3.5 million. Northern Ireland, with a population of 1.6 million and a labour force of almost 700,000, occupies the north-east corner of Ireland.

Measures to assist employment

Jobseekers' Charter
On 17 December 1991, the Employment Service (ES) launched the Jobseekers' Charter which is an initiative specifically designed to improve the service at local employment offices and to help the unemployed find work as quickly as possible. It is part of the government's initiative known as the Citizen's Charter, and aims to provide a better relationship between client and agency. It was drawn up after consultation with staff in local and area offices and staff in Employment Service headquarters.

Under the standards set by the Charter, ES has to make its commitment to the clients clear and to tell them what they can expect from them. 'The public will know exactly what standards of service they can expect...and what to do if they are unhappy about the service they receive', said the Employment Secretary, speaking at the 1991 launch of the Charter at a London jobcentre. The onus is then on the client to share the responsibility of looking for work, in order to gain the most from ES facilities.

Information will be easily available to the public, being displayed at every jobcentre on a Client Service Board, and will explain what the Charter hopes to achieve, for example:

- upper limits for the time someone has to wait to be seen;
- upper limits for the time it takes to answer the telephone;
- overall standards of promptness and accuracy of benefit payments.

If clients are not satisfied with the service, a complaints procedure has been introduced that is designed to put things right as quickly and easily as possible. In keeping with a more professional and personal service, staff in the Employment Service will wear identity badges and use their names when answering the phone.

The ES has stated through the Charter its commitment to helping the unemployed get back to work. All local offices will work out their own targets for customer service, along with targets for the future, which will be displayed in each office. Performance against local standards will be regularly reviewed to let the public know how well these targets are being met. The Jobseekers' Charter initiative is the first stage in a programme of continual improvement of the ES.

Job Review Workshops and Job Search Seminars

Job Review Workshops began in June 1991 as a pilot and the scheme became national in February 1992. The workshops aim to help people who have been unemployed for around 13 weeks, and who are unlikely to return to their previous employment, to make informed choices about alternative careers by giving them occupational guidance. Workshops last two days and are offered to people after they have been unemployed for three months. They have proved particularly helpful to unemployed managers, professionals and executives. Participants have access to typing, photocopying and telephone facilities and are also provided with stamps and stationery to assist them in looking for work. Job search seminars are designed to encourage participants to widen their search for a job and to improve their techniques in looking for work.

Both seminars and workshops are funded by the Employment Service (ES) and are run by ES staff or external organizations on behalf of the ES. During 1991/2, 90,000 seminar places were available, resulting in 5717 people starting a job, training or employment programme, or other option. In 1992/3, 130,000 places will be available. Over the two-day course, participants undertake a personal audit of skills, qualifications and experience. They use an interactive computerized guidance system to match their working preferences with suitable jobs and are able to research entry routes into particular professions and training facilities. Participants also draw up a comprehensive action plan.

Benefits of the UK economy

Language
The most apparent advantage, one oft-repeated by American companies with operations in the UK, is that Britain offers an English-speaking European base, eliminating the difficulties of language differences.

Business law
British company law does not discriminate against non-British companies, but rather operates an open-door policy. There are no exchange control regulations affecting the movement of money in and out, so profits can be freely repatriated.

Free ports
There are four sites within the UK designated as free ports, within which imported goods may be stored or processed duty free for re-exportation to destinations outside the EC. Most free ports are linked to seaports, while the Birmingham and Belfast free ports are linked to their nearby airports.

Labour force
Labour costs for Britain's workforce of 28 million people have remained low, about 30 per cent less than those in the USA, approximately 45 per cent lower than Germany and more than 20 per cent below those in France and Italy. The UK's responsive workforce has tallied record levels of productivity. Since 1980, productivity in Britain has risen an impressive 51 per cent.

Health costs
While American health insurance rates are soaring – and creating a financial crisis for many employer-providers – Britain's government-funded health care is available without charge under its National Health Service.

Taxes
The UK's corporate tax rate, at 35 per cent, is among the lowest in industrialized countries. The small-company rate is 25 per cent, for businesses with taxable profits under £100,000. The UK tax system offers generous allowances for capital expenditures, including:

- 100 per cent allowances for trade-related expenditures or scientific research;
- 100 per cent allowances for the construction of industrial and commercial buildings in designated Enterprise Zones;

- 25 per cent allowances for investment in plant and machinery; and
- indefinite postponement of reinvested capital gains through 'rollover relief'.

From April 1992 individuals can get tax relief on the payments they make for vocational training. Tax relief is available for training which can lead to a NVQ or SVQ up to and including level 4. NVQs and SVQs are made up of 'units of competence' and any unit qualifies for the relief. Individuals can claim the relief for any unit or part of a NVQ or SVQ even if they are not studying for the full qualification. Relief, however, does not extend to general educational qualifications such as GCSEs, A-levels, (standard grades and Highers in Scotland), even where they are taken as a preliminary to NVQ or SVQ study.

The relief is given on:

- study, examination and registration fees;
- fees payable for assessment purposes, including assessment of prior learning;
- payment for any award or certificate obtained.

It is not given on payments for equipment or textbooks, or the cost of travelling or subsistence in connection with the training.

The tax relief is received directly on payment of course fees by deducting an amount equal to the basic rate of tax from the full fee. For example, if the cost of a training course is £1000 and the basic rate of income tax is 25 per cent, a trainee will pay only £750.

Financial incentives

Britain offers an attractive package of government grants and incentives to encourage industrial development in the country.

The most generous incentives are available to support investment in those areas badly in need of new industry to revitalize their economies. Known collectively as Assisted Areas, they include parts of England, Scotland, Wales and the whole of Northern Ireland, which has the highest levels of financial assistance.

The principal investment incentive is Regional Selective Assistance, available for both manufacturing and service industry projects, and usually based on capital expenditure and the number of jobs to be created or maintained.

Some 25 Enterprise Zones have been created throughout the UK offering companies special benefits that include 100 per cent capital allowances and exemption from local property taxes (business rates) on industrial and commercial buildings.

Additional incentives made available to companies at local levels often include tax-free grants for machinery, employee training, interest relief, rent and research and development projects.

FINDING EMPLOYMENT

EC nationals have the right to live and work in England, Scotland, Wales and Northern Ireland without a work permit. However, a work permit is required for employment in the Isle of Man and the Channel Islands. A full EC passport is required to work in the UK; a visitor's passport or excursion document is not sufficient. EC nationals are free to enter the UK for up to six months to look for work or set up a business. Visitors who intend to stay for longer have to apply for a residence permit on an EEC1 form. These are available from the Immigration and Nationality Office.

EC nationals working in the UK (except in the Isle of Man or the Channel Islands) have the same rights as UK nationals with regard to pay, working conditions, access to housing, vocational education and training, social security and trade union membership. The Employment Service runs a network of jobcentres throughout the UK and free access to these is available for any EC national. Jobcentres can advise on job vacancies and on finding work, as well as provide more general advice on training opportunities. They can be found in all major towns and cities in the UK. To find the address of the nearest office look in *Yellow Pages* or in a local Thomson's directory.

Private employment agencies are a useful source of temporary and, in some sectors (such as the computing industry and hotel and catering), of permanent employment. Their addresses and telephone numbers can be found in *Yellow Pages*. They are usually listed under employment agencies, recruitment agencies, or temporary agencies.

National and regional newspapers are a major source of job advertisements in the UK. National newspapers such as *The Guardian*, *The Times*, *The Independent*, *The Daily Telegraph* and *The Financial Times* all carry job advertisements. In general, these newspapers feature the more professional appointments such as law, teaching, publishing, social work and computing appointments, but many advertise details of local recruitment agencies and job opportunities as well. As far as local newspapers are concerned, Thursday is the main day for job advertisements. There are also many specialist newspapers, journals and magazines. Central, academic, business and careers libraries often hold directories of local journals or Chambers of Commerce publications.

Most employment law and policy in the UK is governed by union agreements or employment legislation. There are no statutory regulations concerning maximum working hours but the average is around

35–39 per week. Similarly, employers have no statutory obligations to provide holiday pay but the norm is around 23 days per year. Most employers honour public holidays as well. There is no statutory minimum wage. There is no legal requirement for employers to recognize trade unions either for negotiations or representation, but dozens of unions do exist and negotiate on behalf of the workforce in many institutions. Many are affiliated to the national umbrella body, the Trades Union Congress (TUC). There is no legal requirement for works councils and very few exist.

INFORMATION POINTS

Education and training

Association for Management
Education and Development
21 Catherine Street
London WC2B 5JS

British Association for Commercial
and Industrial Education (BACIE)
16 Park Crescent
London W1N 4AP

Central Bureau for Educational
Visits and Exchanges
Seymour Mews House
Seymour Mews
London W1H 9PE

Department for Education
Sanctuary Buildings
Great Smith Street
London SW1 3BT

Educational Counselling and Credit
Transfer Service (ECCTIS)
Fulton House
Jessop Avenue
Cheltenham
Gloucs GL50 3SH

ERASMUS Student Grants Council
The University
Canterbury
Kent CT2 7PD

FE Euro Network, Association of
Vocational Colleges International
Middlesex University
White Hart Lane
Tottenham
London N17 8HR

Institute of Training and
Development (ITD)
Marlow House
Institute Road
Marlow
Bucks SL7 1BN

National Council for Vocational
Qualifications (NCVQ)
222 Euston Road
London NW1 2BZ

Post-graduate Awards Department
Department for Education
Mowden Hall
Staindrop Road
Darlington DL3 9BG

Scottish Vocational Education
Council (SCOTVEC)
Hanover House
24 Douglas Street
Glasgow G2 7NQ

Scottish Institute of Adult and
Continuing Education (SIACE)
30 Rutland Square
Edinburgh EH1 2BW

Teacher Training Central Register
and Clearing House
3 Crawford Road
London W1H 2BN

TEMPUS
The British Council
Medlock Street
Manchester M15 4PR

Training and Development Lead
Body (TDLB)
81 Dean Street
London W1V 5AB

Universities Central Council on
Admissions (UCCA)
PO Box 28
Cheltenham
Gloucs GL50 3SA

Employment

The British Council
10 Spring Gardens
London SW1A 2BN

The British Overseas Trade Board
Department of Trade and Industry
Kingsgate House
66–74 Victoria Street
London SW1E 6SW

Business in the Community
227a City Road
London EC1V 1LX

Commission for Racial Equality
(CRE)
Elliott House
10–12 Allington Street
London SW1 5EH

Controller of Social Security
32 La Motte Street
St Helier
Jersey

Department of Employment
Moorfoot
Sheffield S1 4PQ

Department of Employment
Training Policy Branch
Caxton House
Tothill Street
London SW1 9NF

Department of Social Security
Overseas Branch
Newcastle upon Tyne NE98 1YX

Department of Trade and Industry
Ashdown House
123 Victoria Street
London SW1E 6RB

Equal Opportunities Commission
(EOC)
Overseas House
Quay Street
Manchester M3 3HN

European Work Experience
Kipling House
43 Villiers Street
London WC2N 6NE

Exports to Europe Branch
Department of Trade and Industry
Kingsgate House
66–74 Victoria Street
London SW1E 6SW

Foreign and Commonwealth Office
London SW1A 2AH

Immigration and Nationality
Lunar House
40 Wellesley House
Croydon CR9 2BY

Institute of Personnel Management
(IPM)
IPM House
Camp Road
Wimbledon
London SW19 4UX

International Voluntary Service (IVS)
Old Hall
East Bergholt
Colchester
Essex CO7 6TQ

Isle of Man Government
Employment Exchange
Nobles Hall
Westmoreland Road
Douglas
Isle of Man

Labour and Welfare Committee
Bordage House
7–9 The Bordage
St Peter Port
Guernsey

Scottish Business in the Community
Romano House
43 Station Road
Corstorphine
Edinburgh EH12 7AF

Trades Union Congress (TUC)
Congress House
22–28 Great Russell Street
London WC1B 3LS

UK LINGUA unit
Seymour Mews House
London W1H 9PE

Voluntary Service Overseas (VSO)
317 Putney Bridge Road
London SW15 2PN

European Information Centres

Belfast
Local Enterprise Development Unit
Euro Info Centre
Ledu House
Upper Galwally
Belfast BT8 4TB

Birmingham
Birmingham Chamber of Industry
and Commerce
Euro Info Centre
75 Harborne Road
PO Box 360
Birmingham B15 3DH

Bradford
(antenne/Satellite UK-560)
West Yorkshire European Business
Information Centre
Bradford Enterprise Centre
Britannia House
Broadway
Bradford BD1 1JF

Brighton
Federation of Sussex Industries and
Chamber of Commerce
Euro Info Centre
Seven Dials
Brighton BN1 3JS

Bristol
Bristol Chamber of Commerce and
Industry
Euro Info Centre
16 Clifton Park
Bristol BS8 3BY

Cardiff
Wales Euro Info Centre
Guest Building
PO Box 430
Cardiff CF1 3XT

Exeter
Exeter Enterprises Ltd
University of Exeter
Euro Info Centre
Hailey Wing
Reed Hall
Exeter EX4 4QR

Glasgow
Scottish Enterprise
Euro Info Centre
Atrium Court
50 Waterloo Street
Glasgow G2 6HQ

Inverness
Highland Opportunity Ltd
Development Department
Highland Regional Council
Euro Info Centre
Regional Buildings
Glenurquhart Road
Inverness IV3 5NX

Leeds
Euro Info Centre Yorkshire and
Humberside
Westgate House
100 Wellington Street
Leeds LS1 4LT

Leicester
The Leicester EIC Partnership
Euro Info Centre
Business Advice Centre
30 New Walk
Leicester LE1 6TF

Liverpool
North West Euro Service Ltd
Liverpool City Libraries
William Brown Street
Liverpool L3 8EW

London
London Chamber of Commerce and
Industry
Euro Info Centre
69 Cannon Street
London EC4N 5AB

Small Firms Service
Centre for European Business
Information
11 Belgrave Road
London SW1V 1RB

European Vocational Education Systems

Maidstone
Kent County Council Economic
Development Department
Kent European Information Centre
County Hall
Maidstone ME14 1XQ

Manchester
Manchester Chamber of Commerce
and Industry
Euro Info Centre
56 Oxford Street
Manchester M60 7HJ

Newcastle
Northern Development Company
North of England Euro Info Centre
Great North House
Sandyford Road
Newcastle upon Tyne NE1 8ND

Norwich
Norwich and Norfolk Chamber of
Commerce and Industry
European Information Centre East
Anglia
112 Barrack Street
Norwich NR3 1UB

Nottingham
Nottingham Chamber of Commerce
and Industry
Euro Info Centre
First Floor, South Block
309 Haydn Road
Nottingham NG5 1DG

Slough
Thames Chiltern Chamber of
Commerce and Industry
Euro Info Centre
Commerce House
2–6 Bath Road
Slough SL1 3SB

Stafford
(antenne/Satellite UK-569)
Staffordshire Development
Association
Staffordshire European Business
Centre
3 Martin Street,
Stafford ST16 2LH

Southampton
The Southern Area
European Information Centre
Civic Centre
Southampton SO9 4XP

Telford
Shropshire Chamber of Commerce
and Industry
Euro Info Centre
Industry House
Halesfield 20
Telford TF7 4TA

Chapter 14

EC Schemes Promoting Access to Vocational Training

The main EC training programmes are described below:

COMETT (COMMUNITY ACTION PROGRAMME FOR EDUCATION AND TRAINING IN TECHNOLOGY)

COMETT is a European network of universities and training partnerships which help companies organize training programmes and university enterprise exchanges for staff, trainees and trainers with those in other Member States. Since 1990 the COMETT programme has opened its doors to the EFTA countries (European Free Trade Association). COMETT is working to develop a European infrastructure by setting up a network of University Enterprise Training Partnerships (UETPs). Serving as links between universities and industry, these partnerships identify and respond to the training needs and resources in a given sector or region by developing specific projects and activities. It involves cooperation between universities and industry regarding training in advanced technology, especially in response to technological change. The programme is aimed at persons who have completed their initial training as well as those in active employment.

COMETT encourages cross-border interchange of students and university graduates, scientists and specialists.

Through the project many measures to promote continuing training in the technology sector have been implemented, as well as developments in the field of multi-media distance education. The UETPs form the backbone of the COMETT programme. There are two main types of UETP:

- Regional UETPs: they bring together within a particular geographical area groups of higher education institutions and groups of enterprises.
- Sectoral UETPs: these partnerships of a transnational character associate higher education institutions and companies within a given technological field or industrial sector.

Several dozen partners are very often involved in a single UETP: universities, colleges, enterprises, professional associations, etc. Each consortium seeks to:

- identify training needs in the field of technology;
- respond to these specific needs for the training of highly skilled human resources;
- provide a supporting structure for COMETT activities;
- reinforce inter-regional cooperation and exchange among EC Member States and EFTA countries.

ERASMUS (EUROPEAN ACTION SCHEME FOR THE MOBILITY OF UNIVERSITY STUDENTS)

A scheme which encourages students to spend part of their time studying at an institution in another country, the ERASMUS programme promotes both the mobility of students in the EC and greater cooperation between universities. A large number of students are given the opportunity to complete a recognized part of their course of study in another EC Member State. Support is given to university cooperation programmes, common curricula, intensive educational programmes, study visits by lecturers and administrative personnel, exchange schemes for lecturers, recognized exchange study schemes for students, mutual recognition and diploma study periods, as well as other associated initiatives.

FORCE

The FORCE programme started in 1991 and will run for four years. It is an EC-wide programme to promote continuing vocational education within companies. A number of factors have convinced Member State governments of the need to adopt such a programme, in particular, increased world competition, labour market developments and demographic trends. The EC firmly believes that continuing training and education while in employment has a key role to play in the acheivements of the internal market. As a result of the FORCE programme, investment in continuing vocational training by enterprises is on the increase throughout the Community.

There is danger, however, that training being developed in firms is piecemeal, answering only short-term objectives of immediate skills gaps instead of longer-term goals of raising the skills level in general.

FORCE will try to remedy this through its programme of sectoral analysis and forecasting of trends in qualifications and jobs.

IRIS

The IRIS network was launched in 1988 on the initiative of the European Commission. IRIS falls within the intersection of the Commission's Task Force on Human Resources, Education, Training and Youth, and the Equal Opportunities Unit. The IRIS network is called upon to act as an ambassador to ensure that women's training has a place on the political agenda. It traverses other EC training networks, ensuring a greater presence of women trainees on their courses and helping to develop EC training policies. IRIS cuts across boundaries of sector, level of skill, age, experience and occupational status to focus on the specific needs of women.

How IRIS works

The Commission finances the IRIS network and has overall responsibility for it. CREW (Centre for Research on European Women), an independent organization, is repsonsible for the general coordination of IRIS and the everyday management of its work. The Member States also have an important input in IRIS, as members of the Commission's Working Group on Vocational Training for Women.

IRIS member programmes exchange information among themselves. They are linked on a national and a European level. They can participate in all IRIS general activities and can apply for its grants.

IRIS activities

The IRIS network offers a wide variety of services and activities aimed at promoting women's training and at building links between training programmes for women, the social partners and government authorities. These activities include:

- contacts with other training programmes for women throughout the European Community;
- information distribution;

- possibilities for transnational partnerships and cooperation through its partnerships grant scheme;
- inter-programme exchange visits to selected IRIS training programmes throughout the community;
- publicity grants for model programmes;
- an on-line IRIS database with regularly updated information on members;
- publications, including the IRIS bulletin with up-to-date news on training initiatives and about the network, IRIS seminar dossiers and other specialized dossiers;
- the annual IRIS membership directory;
- a computerized electronic mail and bulletin board;
- the IRIS European Training Fairs, with major exhibitions including the work of model IRIS programmes, workshops and cultural activities.

IRIS members

IRIS member programmes represent a wide spectrum, from small women's workshops to large government-run programmes. Together they train thousands of women throughout the European Community: women who want to return to work, those who are just starting out and those already in jobs, seeking promotion or change. Membership of IRIS has grown since its launch in 1988 when there were 71 founder members; it now has over 450 member training programmes throughout the Community.

IRIS programmes provide training in a wide variety of sectors, from new technologies, management and enterprise creation to manual skills and tourism. Although mixed training programmes are eligible for membership of the network – if they make specific provision for women trainees – most member programmes train women only. The biggest target age group is 25–40 years, followed by the 18–25 age group, with relatively few programmes providing training for very young women (16–18 years). IRIS's main target groups are women returners and long-term unemployed women, though the network also contains programmes providing various types of in-service training.

LINGUA (PROGRAMME FOR THE PROMOTION OF FOREIGN LANGUAGE KNOWLEDGE IN THE EUROPEAN COMMUNITY)

The LINGUA programme seeks to improve foreign language teaching

and the learning of foreign languages within the European Community.
The programme is aimed at:

- language teachers who wish to increase their professional
  competence;
- universities and institutions that train language teachers;
- students who are studying foreign languages;
- institutions which offer foreign language courses for the business and
  vocational sectors;
- institutions that promote educational initiatives and exchange
  schemes for young people between 16 and 25 years of age (especially
  as a part of vocational training).

NOW (NEW OPPORTUNITIES FOR WOMEN)

NOW, costing ECU 120 million, was launched in December 1990 and is
directed exclusively at projects for women. It aims to contribute to
equality of opportunity for women in employment and vocational
training. The measures, which may be jointly financed by the Member
States and the EC's structural funds, include the following:

- creation of small enterprises and cooperatives by women;
- training and support measures to help women find employment;
- supplementary measures such as the setting up of day nurseries,
  particularly in industrial areas. Technical measures have also been
  included, such as assistance with the setting up or extension of
  support structures, awareness projects, transfer of personnel,
  trainers, trainees and experience.

PETRA

PETRA was launched in 1990, and is concerned with vocational training
for young people and their preparation for working life. It operates
through a network of training initiatives based in each Member State.
The PETRA programme can help to fund exchanges. The PETRA 11
programme came into force on 1 January 1992, and has been allocated
a budget of ECU 177.4 million. The programme is intended for young
people up to age 28 who are in one of the following situations:

- receiving initial vocational education;
- in employment or available on the labour market who have not
  received initial vocational training or practical work experience; and
- those who have completed initial vocational training and who are
  taking part in an advanced programme to complete their training.

It should be noted that 'initial vocational training' is used to denote any form of non-university initial vocational training, including technical vocational training and apprenticeships, which enable young people to gain a recognized vocational qualification.

TEMPUS (TRANS-EUROPEAN MOBILITY SCHEME FOR UNIVERSITY STUDIES FOR CENTRAL AND EASTERN EUROPEAN COUNTRIES)

TEMPUS supports businesses and higher education in carrying out training projects with similar organizations in other European countries. Included in the programme are the exchange of teachers, trainers, trainees and students, and mobility grants for teachers and students. Under TEMPUS projects may be linked, as appropriate, to existing networks, notably those funded in the framework of the ERASMUS, COMETT and LINGUA programmes.

Appendices

1. EUROPEAN COMMUNITY ADDRESS LIST

COMETT
COMETT Technical Assistance Unit
rue Montoyer 14
1040 Brussels

Commission of the EC – Task Force
Human Resources, Education,
Training and Youth
rue de la Loi, 200
1049 Brussels

CEDEFOP – European Centre for the
Development of Vocational Training
Jean Monnet House
Bundesallee 22
1000 Berlin 15

ERASMUS
Erasmus Bureau
rue Montoyer 70
1040 Brussels

EUROQUALIFICATION
Permanent Transnational Technical
Assistance Team
rue Duquesnoy 38 – Box 13
1000 Brussels

FORCE
Bat Force
rue de Nord 34
1000 Brussels

IRIS
CREW
rue de la Tourelle 21
1040 Brussels

LINGUA
LINGUA Bureau
rue du Commerce 10
1040 Brussels

NOW
Equal Opportunities Unit
Commission of the European
Communities
Directorate General V – B.4
rue de la Loi 200
1049 Brussels

Office for Official Publications of
the European Communities
2, rue Mercier
2985 Luxembourg

PETRA
Petra-Ifaplan
Square Ambiorix 32
1040 Brussels

TEMPUS
Tempus office
rue Montoyer 14
1040 Brussels

2. NATIONAL ACADEMIC RECOGNITION INFORMATION CENTRES (NARIC)

Belgium

Ministere de l'Education Nationale
Services des equivalences de
l'enseignement superieur
Direction generale de l'Ensiegnement
superieur et de la Recherche
scientifique – 1ere Direction – CAE
Quartier des Arcades/6eme etage
rue Loyale 204
1010 Brussels

Ministerie van Onderwijs
Bestuur van het Hoger Onderwijs en
Wetenschappelijk Onderzoek
Dienst Gelijkwaardigheid
Manhatten Center, Toren 2
Kruisvaartenstraat 3
1210 Brussels

Denmark

NARIC
Undervisningsministeriet
Det internationale kontor
Frederiksholms Kanal 25 D
1220 Kopenhavn K

France

Ministere de l'Education Nationale
Direction des affaires generales,
internationales et de la Cooperation
DAGIC 8
Bureau d'information, de
documentation et de soutien aux
etablissments
110 rue de Grenelle
75007 Paris

Germany

Sekretariat der Standigen Konferenz
der Kultusminister der Lander
Zentralstelle fur auslandisches
Bildungswesen
Nassestrasse 8
5300 Bonn 1

Greece

DIKATSA
Inter-University Centre for the
Recognition of Foreign Academic
Titles
112 Leoforos Syngrou
11741 Athens

Ireland

Higher Education Authority
21 Fitzwilliam Square
Dublin

Italy

Centro di Informazione sulla
Mobilita e le Equivalenze
Accademiche
CIMEA
Fondazione RUI
Viale XXI Aprile 36
00162 Roma

Luxembourg

Ministere de l'Education Nationale
et de la Jeunesse
Centre d'information sur la
reconnaissance academique des
diplomas et des periodes d'etudes
6 boulevard Royal
2449 Luxembourg

The Netherlands

National Equivalence Information
Centre (NEIC)
Nederlandse Organisatie voor
Internationale Samenwerking in het
Hoger
Onderwijs 251
2609s Gravenhage

Portugal

Ministerio da Educação e Cultura
Direcção-Geral do Ensino Superior
Centro de Informação sobre
Reconhecimento Academico de
Diplomas
(CIRAD)
Av 5 de Outubro 107–9
1051 Lisboa, Codex

Spain

Ministerio de Educacion y Ciencia
Subdireccion General de
Cooperacion Internacional
Centro de Informacion sobre
Reconocimiento de Titulos y
Movilidad de Estudiantes
Paseo del Prado 28, 4a planta
28014 Madrid

United Kingdom

National Academic Recognition
Information Centre (NARIC)
The British Council
10 Spring Gardens
London SW1A 2BN

3. COMPARABILITY COORDINATORS

Belgium

M Bustin/CAE Arcades
Ministére de l'Education Nationale –
d4542
bd Pacheco 19 Bte 0
1040 Bruxelles

J Clarys
Vlaamse Ministerie van Onderwijs
Molenstraat 22
8930 Boezinge Ieper

Denmark

Birgit Bududu
Undervisningsministerium
H C Andersens Boulevard 43
1553 Kobenhaven V

France

Mme Maurage
Delegation à la Formation
Professionnelle
50–56 rue de la Procession
75015 Paris

Germany

Bundesministerium für Bildung und
Wissenschaft
Bonn
Germany

Greece

Dr N Iliadis
Paidagogiko Institouto
Mesogeion Avenue 396
15 341 Athens

European Vocational Education Systems

Mmes A Georgiadou/
E Constantacopoulou
Ypourgio Pedias & Politismou
Metropoleos Street
10 185 Athens

Ireland

Mr John Reilly
Department of Labour
65a Adelaide Road
Dublin 2

Italy

Dr N Fiore
Direttore Generale
Ufficio Centrale OFPL
Ministero del Lavoro
Via Castelfidardo 43
00185 Roma

Luxembourg

Pierre Wiseler
Directeur à la Formation
Professionnelle
29 rue Aldringen
2926 Luxembourg

The Netherlands

COLO Centraal Orgaan
Van de Landelijke
Opleidingsorganen
AG Zoetermeer

Portugal

Fernando Cabecinha
Instituto do Emprego e Formação
Professional
Rua Xabregas 52
1900 Lisbon

Spain

Hilario Mesa Fernández
Instituto Nacional de Empleo
C/ Condesa de venadito 9
28027 Madrid

United Kingdom

The Comparability Coordinator
Employment Department
Qualifications and Standards Branch
– QS1
Room E603
Moorfoot
Sheffield S1 4PQ

4. EC LAWS

It is helpful to be familiar with the procedures by which the European
Community proposes legislation. In broad terms:

* The Commission (which has both executive and administrative roles)
  initiates and drafts proposals and submits them to the Council.
* The European Parliament (whose 518 members are elected every five
  years by the citizens of the European Community) is consulted either
  under the Consultation Procedure or the Cooperation Procedure.
  The Parliament has the power to propose amendments and under the
  Cooperation Procedure can overrule the Commission and the
  Council if it can command an absolute majority (260 out of 518).

- The Economic and Social Committee (ECOSOC) consists of 189 members who represent employers' organizations and other interest groups in all 12 Member States. ECOSOC is consulted mainly on social and economic proposals.
- The Council consists of Government representatives from the 12 Member States, normally Ministers. When a proposal is adopted by the Council, it becomes European Community law.

Outlined below are the different types of Community measures in use.

Directives

A Directive is a European Community law binding on the Member States as to the result to be achieved, but leaving the choice of method open to each. In most cases, this requires national implementing legislation to be approved by the parliament of each Member State in accordance with the customs and procedure of that Member State. This is an important point as businesses affected by a Directive have to take account of national implementing legislation as well as the Directive itself. There can be a substantial time gap between approval of a Directive by the Council and its implementation into the national law of all 12 Member States.

Regulations

A Regulation is a law which is binding and directly applicable in all Member States without requiring any implementing national legislation. Both the Council and the Commission can adopt Regulations.

Decisions

Decisions can be issued either by the Council or by the Commission. They are binding on those to whom they are addressed. No national implementing legislation is required. A Decision may be addressed to a Member State, to a company or to an individual. A Decision which involves financial penalties or similar obligations is enforceable in national courts.

Recommendations and Opinions

Neither Recommendations nor Opinions have any binding effect; they are not laws. They state the view of the institution that issues them and they may urge action. They can be issued by both the Council and the Commission, though generally by the latter.

Index